THROUGH
THE EYES OF GOD

I Am Fearfully and Wonderfully Made

SHEILA L. JACKSON

Through the Eyes of God
by Sheila L. Jackson
Copyright ©2009 Sheila L. Jackson

Scriptures marked KJV are taken from the *King James Version* of the Bible. Scriptures marked TLB are taken from *The Living Bible* by Kenneth N. Taylor, Used by permission of Tyndale House, Wheaton, IL. Scripture quotations are taken from *THE HOLY BIBLE: New International Version* ©1978 by the New York International Bible Society, used by permission of Zondervan Bible Publishers. Scriptures marked MSG are taken from *THE MESSAGE*. Copyright © by Eugene H. Peterson 1993, 1994, 1995, 1996, 2000, 2002. Used by permission of NavPress Publishing Group. Scriptures marked AMP are taken from *The Amplified Bible,* Old Testament. Copyright 1965, 1987, by The Zondervan Corporation. All are used by permission. All rights reserved.

ISBN 978-1-58169-342-3
For Worldwide Distribution
Printed in the U.S.A.

Axiom Press
P.O. Box 191540 • Mobile, AL 36619
800-367-8203

To my mother, Mary L. Lewis,

thanks for sacrificing your needs and wants,

so that your girls' needs could be meet.

You taught me how to be the strong woman

that I am today and to stand

on my own two feet.

Acknowledgments

I would like to thank my Lord and Savior, Jesus Christ, because He has anointed me with the gift to write and to share His Word with the world.

A big hug and kisses to my husband, Timothy and daughters, Brittany and Amber. Thanks for supporting my dreams and helping lug my book signing equipment and materials to every event. I know it gets tiresome at times, but you keep hanging in there with me.

To my pastor, James T. Sims and the Lake Zion Church family, I thank you from the bottom of my heart for the sincere love and support that you have shown me in my writing endeavors. I am so blessed and proud to be a part of a church family that cares for one another. To Cassandra Dennis and Kathy Sheppard, you two have been instrumental in getting my book to circulate in the North Caddo area. I pray that God has a special blessing on both your lives because you promoted my book as if it was your own. Cassandra, I have so much love and respect for you as a woman of God because you continued to promote my book when your daughter was battling cancer at St. Jude. Truly it took great strength and faith to think of others while in the midst of your trial.

Special thanks go to Apostle Cornell Hamilton, overseer of From Bondage to Freedom Outreach Ministries. You and your congregation went over and above to help support and promote my book. You gave up thirty minutes of your radio air-time on numerous days so that I could introduce my book to the Ark-La-Tex area. I will never forget the kindness that was shown towards me.

Pastor James Green, Coach (Union Mission Baptist Church), Pastor Jimmy Carroll (Greater Mt. Nebo Baptist Church), Bishop Jerry L. Maiden (Church of the Living God), Pastor Daniel Washington (New Beginning Faith Tabernacle Baptist Church), Pastor Morris Austin (Mt. Canaan Baptist Church), and The Lane Chapel CME Church family along with other ministries—thanks for inviting me into your church homes to promote my book.

My gratitude to Alvin Moore at Comcast Cable, KTBS-3 Shreveport, Barbara Norton at KOKA, and Ivy Latin (public relations) at the Shreveport Libraries, without these entities it would have been difficult to get the word out about my book.

Thanks a million to the Herndon Middle Magnet School faculty for inviting me to take part in honoring and naming your magnet program after the late Barbara L. Jefferson with a book signing—in her memory.

Lastly, my appreciation and gratitude goes out my agent/author coach, Keith Carroll, and Axiom Press, and to all those that have supported me by buying my books and encouraging your friends and family to do likewise. Thank you for believing in what God has anointed me to do—share His Word.

Table of Contents

Introduction

If you would just take a moment out of your busy schedule to watch and observe the people that you come in contact with from day to day, you might see that many of them are suffering from depression, an identity crisis, and/or weight issues. You do not have to be a psychologist to realize that something has gone terribly wrong in the world in which you live. More than ever, people are confused as to who they are and what is considered to be beautiful. Even the television shows and magazines are consumed with issues of this nature. You see what the world wants you to see and feel about yourself. You have been programmed and brainwashed into the world's system of beauty.

Drug addicts and alcoholics in Hollywood are setting false examples of what real beauty is, when in reality, most of them are not happy with who they are. If they were, rehabilitation centers would not be accepting them at an alarming rate.

We have allowed celebrities who are breaking the law, driving drunk, having babies out of wedlock, engaging in high profile infidelity, pill popping, and getting intoxicated to set the standards of beauty for us. Has anyone taken notice? These are the things that are captivating our young impressionable kids. They are growing up in a society that cares more about their rib cages showing through their skin than looking healthy and fit. These are the images that our children are being exposed to everyday, and we wonder why they are dying to be thin, hip, and cool. What they see when they are looking at their favorite celebrities are those who are starving themselves with unsuccessful fad diets or causing themselves to vomit so they can fit into a size zero.

Society has become overly obsessed with self-image until it has resulted in people taking extreme measures to be perfect and to meet standards that are unobtainable. In the past, it appeared as though women were the only ones that struggled with a low self-image, but today men are quickly following the trail behind them.

Why can't we see ourselves as God does? We are beautiful just the way we are. True, we all want to better ourselves or to change something about our appearances. Although as we grow in Christ, change is expected of us, that change is inward.

God loves your big hips, your thick or thin lips, your straight or nappy hair, big or small body frame, and white or black, red or yellow complexion. He loves you. You are His creation, His masterpiece, designed for His pleasure and enjoyment. God did not waste His time when He sculpted and molded you in His image. So, why have you allowed man to tell you that you are less than God's best?

> *But you are not like that, for you have been chosen by God himself—you are priests of the King, you are holy and pure, you are God very own— all this so that you may show to others how God called you out of the darkness into his wonderful light. Once you were less than nothing; now you are God's own. Once you knew very little of God's kindness; now your very lives have been changed by it* (I Peter 2:9-10, TLB).

Do not allow people to make you feel as though you are nothing. God has called you out to be so much more—more than what you could ever imagine for yourself. When people try to make you feel small and unimportant, know that such a lie is one of Satan's tricks. He uses those who are closest to you to make you look at yourself in a negative way. Whatever negative comments people make about you and your appearance, remember that God said, "You are not like that." He sees the beauty and the potential that lies beneath the poor self-image that you have of yourself. When God called you into a royal priesthood, He wanted you to know what you are worth to Him. He has chosen you to be the peculiar one—strange to the world but unique to Him.

Your thinning hairline down to the rolls on your belly are no accidents to God. He knew what He wanted you to look like before you were born. He did not plan on everyone looking exactly the same. You are skipping meals and overexercising to fit an image that someone else has chosen for you. Each time you look into the mirror at yourself, you sink further and further into depression. In your mind, you feel that you do not measure up to everyone else. If the truth be told, no one measures up to man's standards, and neither does the man or woman who set those unobtainable standards.

We are a society that has become consumed with beauty and perfection until we have forgotten who the only perfect One really is —Jesus. No one will ever top the perfect Lamb of God. We may snip, tuck, and clip parts of our body; but we will never reach perfection as long as we live here on earth.

Measure your self-worth and beauty by God's standards. Man's standards will cause you to have low self-esteem issues and feelings of inadequacy. It may even cause you to have suicidal thoughts. But the person that sees him or herself as God does, sees him or herself as beautiful even though they may have flaws. Their imperfection does not control the way they see themselves.

You are a diamond in the rough. There is no one exactly like you—the mold was broken when you were created. Only when you see yourself as God sees you will you love the image that you see staring back at you in the mirror. You will never see yourself as beautiful or unique until you can see yourself clearly through the eyes of God.

I praise you because I am

fearfully and wonderfully made;

your works are wonderful,

I know that full well.

(Psalms 139:14 KJV)

Chapter One

Identity Crisis

But by the grace of God I am what I am: and his grace which was bestowed upon me was not in vain (1 Corinthians 15:1 KJV).

Kim was taught by her parents that she was perfect just the way she was. But at the age of thirteen, she allowed her classmates to tell her a different story. She developed low self-esteem and started experimenting with drugs to fit into what she thought was the cool crowd. Her once normal and perfect life was now shattered because she failed to realize how wonderful and unique she was. After experiencing bouts of poor self-confidence, Kim lost one of the most important aspects of her life—her identity. Because she had conformed into what friends wanted her to be, she struggled throughout her teenage years with confusion about her goals and priorities.

Do you know who you are in Christ? Are you trying to be someone you're not? Perhaps you are uncomfortable in your skin or are belittling others to make yourself feel superior over them. Do you expose the flaws of others to cover up your own or boast about your self-worth, when in reality you are not who you profess to be? If this is you, then you are suffering from what society has labeled as an identity crisis.

Millions of people around the country each year struggle with low self-esteem. Psychologist Stanley Coopersmith in his book, *Antecedents of Self Esteem,* says, "Self-esteem (or self-regard), is an evaluative measure of our self-image." He terms it as a "personal judgment of worthiness that is expressed in the attitudes the individual holds towards himself." He goes on further to say, "These personal evaluations will be based on values of the

1

social groups and the society. When one of the personal characteristics that make up our self-ideal fails to match that corresponding quality, which we, through society's eyes have placed in our ideal self, there is a fall in self-esteem."

An identity crisis begins when an individual is confused about who he or she is as a person. People like this need others to validate them and the things that they do. In other words, because of their lack of confidence in themselves, they need a stamp of approval from others to tell them who they are and should be as people. Identity crises normally begin during the adolescent years. Coopersmith says that an identity crisis begins for children ages eleven to eighteen years and continues throughout their educational lives.

People have traveled across the world in search of their identities and self-fulfillment, needlessly spending thousands of dollars when all they have to do is pick up their Bibles. God's Word will tell them all they need to know about who they are and more. Most black Americans feel as though they must travel to Africa to truly know and understand where they come from and who they are. It helps them to break free from the stereotypes that were placed upon them by their white counterparts. Many white Americans in search of their identities delay college to travel to Europe and abroad in search of self-fulfillment. God is saying, "Ask Me. I created you. I can tell you what you need to know about yourself. I can fulfill anything and everything that is lacking within you. You do not have to travel across the world. I am right here with the answers that you desperately seek."

The way to find your true identity is through Christ. You must first love who He says you are in Him. You can read all the self-help books on the market and talk to as many psychologists that are willing to take your money. But until you are willing to pray to God for the answers concerning your place in this world, you will continue to see yourself as less than best. Jesus is the best therapist for helping you to understand who you are, not a magazine article or television show. The words that He speaks are real and piercing to the soul. No one has the ability or power that is needed for you to see and understand the real you except for Christ. Only His living Word has the ability to empower and change a person's self-perception.

I am what I am. God did not created me in vain; He did not look at me afterwards and say, "I made a mistake; let Me start over again." He knew what He wanted me to look like inside and out before I was born.

Unfortunately we have allowed Satan (through the world's system, which belongs to him) to tell us that something is wrong with the way that we look and how we are built. We begin to doubt who God has created us to be; therefore, we tamper with His masterpiece—our bodies, His clay, His sculpture.

Misery Loves Company

There was a man named Elkanah (see 1 Samuel 1*)* who had two wives, one of which was named Hannah. She could not bear children. The name of the other wife was Peninnah. She had many sons and daughters. In the Bible days, a woman was looked upon as worthless or cursed if she could not procreate. This caused Hannah's spirit to be sorrowful, to the point that she could not eat. She experienced a great deal of depression. To make matters worse, she had an adversary (Peninnah) that taunted her because of her barrenness. *"And her adversary also provoked her sore, for to make her fret, because the Lord had shut up her womb"* (1 Samuel 1:6 KJV). Peninnah wanted to make Hannah feel as miserable as she possibly could. Each year as they traveled to Shiloh to offer sacrifices to the Lord, Peninnah continued mocking Hannah.

I believe that the constant putdowns from Peninnah made Hannah feel worthless. If only she knew that her barrenness did not make her less of a woman. When you allow people to speak negatively into your life, you conform to what is said about you. This was not the case with Hannah.

Women of that day hid themselves in shame, but Hannah did something about her problem. She took it to God. She went to God in prayer and told Him about her situation. God answered her petitions with a son named Samuel.

When people are bullying or belittling others, I believe they do so because they are not happy with themselves. Peninnah knew that Elkanah loved Hannah more than her. This may have been one reason why she tried to make Hannah feel unhappy and depressed about being childless.

Misery loves company. It was true in the Bible days, and it is still true today. Who told you that because you are fat, too skinny, nose too wide, lips too big or thin, and derriere too flat or big that you are not beautiful? Are you less than a person if these body parts are not proportioned according to what society dictates? The people that put these stipulations on the way that you should look have underlining issues within themselves. Will God love you less if you are not a perfect size ten? The answer is no!

If we could see ourselves as Christ sees us, the identity problem that is causing us to doubt who we are as individuals would not exist. When we allow the world to set the standards for us, we stop looking at ourselves through the eyes of God and start looking at ourselves through the eyes of man. In man's eyes are imperfections and constant changes that need to be made on the exterior—a snip here and a tuck there to help those places where God missed, or so man's feeble mind believes.

Why can't we just be ourselves? We live in a society where people want to look like their favorite celebrities. They take pictures to plastic surgeon offices, wanting them to sculpt their bodies and faces into several different celebrities. They want to have J-Lo's behind, Beyounce's curves, Hallie Berry's eyes and nose, Julia Robert's smile, and Angelina Jolie's lips. Mixing all these features together would create a monster. They look good on those individuals, not us. Our features match our bodies and facial types.

True, plastic surgery can enhance not-so-perfect features. But society has taken it to the extreme. The celebrities themselves do not look the way they appear on television and magazines. We can pull any average woman off the street and take a picture of her, airbrushing the photo to make her appear flawless and glamorous. Our favorite celebrities constantly have to reinvent themselves because otherwise their fans would lose their attraction to them. Who wants to live day in and day out worrying about looking picture perfect before going out in public? Did I look too fat when the cameras snapped my picture? Is my hairline receding? Do I have too many wrinkles? Many celebrities live in fear that their fans will lose interest if they look too old or are not as sexy as they once were.

When physical obsession starts to show its ugly head, we begin to put God in the backseat of our lives. We allow Satan's negative opinions of us to take control of how we view ourselves. Everybody wants to be and act like everyone else. No one wants to be like his or her Father—God. We have lost focus of those areas that matter most in our lives. What is wrong with wanting to be like Jesus, caring more that our attributes and characteristics are like His? Why do we make sure that the outward man is dressed to perfection, instead of giving the priority to the inward man? God does not care about our outward appearance. He cares more about our beauty inside and wants us not to become shallow, vain, and condemning of others.

Identity Crisis

As our world becomes more consumed with the outer appearance than what is on the inside of a person, an identity crisis will develop in most people. More than ever, people are conforming themselves to what others want them to be. But God is saying, "By my grace, I have made you who I wanted you to be." In Him, you are complete, because He has molded you in His image. No longer does an identity crisis have to control and destroy your life because God has given you His stamp of approval to be unique.

Chapter Two

Stolen Identity

Jeff Smith was raised on a farm with hard working parents. His father taught him that real men work hard to provide a comfortable lifestyle for their families and that a good name and reputation will earn a man respect. As an adult, Jeff left behind what his father had instilled in him. He had changed after moving to the big city where most people were rude and critical of others. In his new surroundings, his net worth appeared to be more important than his character.

Jeff became caught up in the hustle and bustle to obtain financial wealth, no matter whom he had to step on to achieve it. He allowed fellow colleagues to poison his mind against the employees with lower ranking jobs. They would tell Jeff, "People work these menial jobs because they are lazy and do not want better for themselves and families." Before long, Jeff allowed these men to steal his identity because he bought into their lies. The young man that his father spent time on grooming to be an upstanding citizen was now gone. Jeff did not realize the person that he had become.

Don't become the next case of stolen identity. People know just how to influence you—to do good or evil. You may say to yourself that others cannot control the way that you think. But Jeff is a classic case that if you hang around negative people long enough and participate in the evil conversations of others, the person that your parents raised you to be will become a distant memory.

Loss of Identity as God's People

People have become so busy and obsessed with trying to fit into society's ideal of self-worth that they have lost their compassion for others. Are we becoming a product of this society's identity meltdown? No one is exempt. We have become a part of the problem by stealing the identity of others. We are in trouble because we have lost our identity as people of God. Everyone wants to be, look, and act like everyone else. Our priorities no longer include saving lost souls and helping them understand who they are in Christ Jesus.

We have become so overly consumed with what we have or have not that the spirit of condemnation has taken over us. People that once came to us for solace and spiritual edification are now being told that if they do not look, dress, speak, and act a certain way, they cannot be part of our clique.

We are becoming more and more responsible for destroying the spiritual identity of others. We have left many questioning who they are and where they fit in this cruel world. If people are made to feel that they do not measure up, then where can they go to be edified and spiritually encouraged? The Word of God is about elevating and motivating, not crushing another's self-esteem.

Who are we to judge anyone? Only humble spirits can help promote the spiritual growth of those that have had their dignity stripped away by the lies of the devil.

> *Don't criticize and speak evil about each other, dear brothers. If you do, you will be fighting against God's law of loving one another, declaring it is wrong. But your job is not to decide whether this law is right or wrong, but to obey it. Only he who made the law can rightly judge among us. He alone decides to save us or destroy. So what right do you have to judge or criticize others?* (James 4:11-12 TLB).

God's law was instituted to prevent us from boasting in ourselves and speaking evil of others. If a person decides to challenge God's law of loving one another, then this individual puts himself in a dangerous position. He is saying in his arrogance, "I know more than God, and I have the right to judge anyone that I think is not on my level of prestige."

The face of our society has definitely had a major facelift over the years. The belief that all men are created equal have been placed on hold. As most businesses have moved into the new millennium, they have become more concerned about their net worth and efforts to increase their bottom dollar than they have to develop the character of and benefits to their employees.

Even our community leaders have lost sight of a person's quality as a human being. Most see them as cash mules or a vote for their cause and nothing more, giving these individuals the shaft after they have taken what they wanted from them.

The have-nots are kicked to the curb, while glitz and glamour are promoted and celebrated. People are broken down spiritually and have become emotional wrecks because we have abandoned them. They are frowned upon because of the clothing they wear. They are turned away because they do not fit the profile of what most groups call blessed and highly favored of the Lord. They are ostracized by those that think they are better because of what they have. They are also made to feel like the dirt underneath one's shoes, because they cannot afford the bare necessities of life.

The almighty dollar has blinded many of our spiritual leaders today. The competition to be the first to build a 5,000 to 20,000 seat edifice has blind-sided many of them. They don't seem to care that people in the community have been spiritually broken by life's trials and heartaches. Because of the popularity contests between our community leaders today, they have become preoccupied with building great edifices instead of building men and women's spirits and giving them hope.

God wants those that are chosen to lead to come out of the buildings and go to the hedges and highways to compel those that have been beaten by life to keep going. He wants them to come and have peace and rest in Him. God is saying, "Because you have spent so much time building and enlarging your homes, these roads have become less traveled and people have fallen by the wayside. Your lack of compassion has caused them to lose sight of who they are in Me."

Come unto me, all ye that labour and are heavy laden, and I will give you rest. Take my yoke upon you, and learn of me; for I am meek and lowly in heart: and ye shall find rest unto your souls. For my yoke is easy, and my burden is light (Matthew 11:28-30 KJV).

Jesus' yoke (the Word) is edifying because it is meant to be spiritually liberating. The world's yoke is hard and humiliating. The world uses harsh and criticizing words that put a person into spiritual isolation. These burdened people believe the sharp and condemning words that have been spoken about them. Therefore, it makes them feel spiritually inadequate in their own eyes.

As a uniformed body, we should focus more on healing the negative ways of thinking of those around us, explain to them that their identity has been stolen, and show them how to reclaim it. Yes, our communities are in a state of chaos because we have lost sight of who we are in Christ. We have bought into the superficial world of Hollywood and forced others to do the same if they want to fit in with the rest of the crowd. But Jesus said, *"My yoke is wholesome (useful, good—not harsh, hard, sharp, or pressing, but comfortable, gracious, and pleasant), and My burden is light and easy to be borne"* (Matthew 11:30 AMP).

Why are we trapped in our sense of self? Greed and competition with others are the culprits. Whenever we exalt or esteem ourselves above God—our Creator—we lose touch with who we are. God created you for a specific purpose. However, when you turn away from that purpose and begin to let the world make you believe that you are better than what you really are, your true identity begins to diminish, leaving you unsettled and frustrated.

When people come to us depressed, they shouldn't leave worse than when they came. Often, we are too busy lecturing them about wealth and obtaining earthly treasures than what is truly important. Many have forgotten that these are real life issues that our friends are facing. We make them feel as if they have failed God if they are not driving expensive cars, living in big homes, or working at jobs that provide six figures of yearly income. This leaves them wondering why they are treated so harshly because they don't possess these material items. Rest assured that having the finer things in life cannot provide access into heaven's gates. Only love for one another will gain favor in the sight of a merciful God.

A Christian who doesn't amount to much in this world should be glad, for he is great in the Lord's sight. But a rich man should be glad that his riches mean nothing to the Lord, for he will soon be gone like a flower that has lost its beauty and fades away, withered—killed by the scorching summer sun. So it is with rich men. They will soon die and leave behind all their busy activities (James 1:9-11 TLB).

In those verses, James is not putting down people who are wealthy. Nothing is wrong with desiring the finer things in life. However, God does not want material possessions to have control over us or cause us to snub our noses at those less fortunate than we are. One day we will die, and any accumulated wealth will not go with us.

In many cases, a rich man doesn't understand why he needs God when he has plenty of money in the bank. But for a poor man with nothing but the clothes on his back, his faith in God that one day he will obtain eternal riches is all that he has. God was not saying that a rich man couldn't enter into heaven. He knew that most would think that their wealth made them worthy of special treatment, causing pride in their lives.

We have allowed the spirit of pride and arrogance to enter into our hearts. We have lost sight of the fact that it took a merciful God to send His Son into the world to save sinners like us, so that all could share in His blessings. We have taken God's goodness for granted and have allowed Satan's evil spirits to take over us. The Scripture teaches, *"The fear of the Lord is to hate evil: pride, and arrogancy, and the evil way, and the froward mouth, do I hate"* (Proverbs 8:13 KJV).

The time is now to start edifying, exhorting, and encouraging one another in the Lord. Hezekiah Walker sang a song entitled, "I Need You To Survive." As humans, one of our missions is to help those that are struggling with the spirit of inadequacy. The song talks about hurting others with our words. Yes, you can hurt people with what you say. Any lies that have been spoken about someone, any gossip, or any other unkind words can bring deep hurts or assassinate a person's character. Negative words have a way of making a person feel incomplete inside. When we speak negative words about another individual, we are responsible for stealing that person's identity because we snatched away his or her confidence the moment we began criticizing.

Don't grumble about each other, brothers. Are you yourselves above criticism? For see! The great Judge is coming. He is almost here (James 5:9 TLB).

This verse is saying to let God handle whatever criticizing must be done. Those that refuse to stop criticizing others will be charged with identity theft in God's heavenly court. They will be responsible for not telling

Satan no when he plants evil words against others in their minds. They saw him coming but did nothing to stop him and his cohorts. They heard him speak but did nothing to silence him. They sat back and allowed him to use them to mistreat others who did not measure up to their standards of prosperity.

Have we become the weapons that are responsible for keeping people from seeing themselves as wonderfully made in God's image? If so, we are painting the picture that people are blessed by the way they look, talk, and dress. Consequently, for the people that do not wear the latest designs, speak with an eloquent voice, or look successful, they are made to feel that they are not prosperous. God wants us to know that success and prosperity comes from knowing who He says we are. A few of these characteristics are listed below:

- We are the apple of His eye.
- We are His most treasured and worthy vessels (because His Son Jesus made us worthy).
- We are a peculiar people (odd to the world, but beautiful to Him).
- We are diamonds in the rough (one of a kind).
- We are fearfully and wonderfully made (flawed from the world's perspective, but perfect in God's eyes).

Dear brothers, how can you claim that you belong to the Lord Jesus Christ, the Lord of glory, if you show favoritism to rich people and look down on poor people? If a man comes into your church dressed in expensive clothes and with valuable gold rings on his fingers, and at the same moment another man comes in who is poor and dressed in threadbare clothes, and you make a lot of fuss over the rich man and give him the best seat in the house and say to the poor man, "You can stand over there if you like, or else sit on the floor"—well, judging a man by his wealth shows that you are guided by wrong motives. Listen to me, dear brothers: God has chosen poor people to be rich in faith, and the Kingdom of Heaven is theirs, for that is the gift God has promised to all those who love him. And yet, of the two strangers, you have despised the poor man. Don't you realize that it is usually the rich men who pick on you and drag you into court? And all too often they are the ones who laugh at Jesus Christ, whose noble name you bear (James 2:1-7 TLB).

This is the behavior of those that disguise themselves as godly. People of God should not despise others because of their attire or where they live. Let's not be the one responsible for such an act. Let's not be the one that strips a man of his dignity or causes him to flee in confusion. Let's not be the one that steals another person's identity.

God wants us to love our fellowman as He loved us. *"Yes indeed, it is good when you truly obey our Lord's command, 'You must love and help your neighbors just as much as you love and take care of yourself.' But you are breaking this law of our Lord's when you favor the rich and fawn over them; it is sin"* (James 2:8-9 TLB). There is no room for favoritism with God. All are welcome and called into His abundant grace.

We all are striving towards the same goal. We all have flaws that are covered by the blood of Jesus. No one can justly stand before God and say who is welcome and who is not, because we are all here by the grace of God.

Dear brothers, don't be too eager to tell others their faults, for we all make many mistakes; and when we teachers of the religion, who should know better, do wrong, our punishment will be greater than it would be for others (James 3:1 TLB).

Building mansions that are as large as football stadiums pales in comparison to reaching out and embracing our fallen brothers and sisters who are searching to find themselves. They have fallen prey to identity theft. The longer they are neglected, the tougher it will be for many of them to believe that their Creator loves them. They will continue to search the world for what God has already given them—an identity.

Don't become the next person to fall into this trap. Search God's Holy Word and discover the person that He has created you to be. You do not have to travel across the country to find it. The Bible contains all the information that you need to know about yourself and more. The time has come for you to reclaim your true self and live above the influence of others.

Chapter Three

Damages of the Tongue

So also the tongue is a small thing, but what enormous damage it can do. A great forest can be set on fire by one tiny spark. And the tongue is a flame of fire. It is full of wickedness, and poisons every part of the body. And the tongue is set on fire by hell itself, and can turn our whole lives into a blazing flame of destruction and disaster. Men have trained or can train, every kind of animal or bird that lives and every kind of reptile and fish, but no human being can tame the tongue. It is always ready to pour out its deadly poison. Sometimes it praises our heavenly Father, and sometimes it breaks out into curses against men who are made like God (James 3:5-9 TLB).

The tongue and its deadly poison are responsible for the spiritual and mental damage of many lives. We think that words cannot destroy a person's spirit and soul, but they can—when that person suffers from low self-esteem. People have committed suicide or have gone on killing sprees as a result of the tongue and its deadly poison. All it takes is just one spark to start the fire burning. For those that have been told that they are good for nothing or will never amount to anything, their self-image has been shattered because of this lethal weapon.

How can something that is used to praise God—the tongue—be used to speak evil of others? Who would have thought that something as small as the tongue could cause such devastation in one's life. James, the half-brother of our Lord and Savior, Jesus Christ, wanted us to be aware of the amount of power in the tongue. It has the power to build up a man as well as take him down a notch. The poison of the tongue has been responsible for destroying many people's lives. James was telling us that if this one little part of the body is not tamed, destruction is sure to follow.

When people go through an identity crisis, you can be sure that the tongue of others is to blame. The tongue is responsible for making them feel inferior or worthless. Words cut like a knife. If men and women keep hearing that they will never amount to anything or that they are unattractive, stupid, or a waste to society, they will eventually conform to what is said about them. Over a period of time, words spoken over us can define who we become as people.

The verses in James 3 should be used to encourage us to embrace people that have been tossed away by society and not to send them further into a spiritual depression. Their emotions are fragile, and love and compassion are necessary to help them find their rightful place in this world. We need to teach them that until they can truly see themselves as worthy of God's love, they will continue to let the poison of the tongue speak negativity into their lives.

Removing Self

God wants you to stand with confidence and love the person that you are in Him, but self has to be removed before this can take place. That is why self-esteem, self-love, and self-confidence cannot be the only means to measure how you should think and feel about yourself. These words focus on you and not the person that God says you are. Most people are devastated when their high opinion of themselves crumbles. These words put you before God and others. When self lets you down, you have nothing else on which to lean. Notice how we worry about what others think about us. This tends to happen when we are constantly thinking of self. When we deny self and put God as the head of our lives, we have Him to rely on when circumstances do not go as planned.

Scripture teaches us to put the concerns and feelings of others above our own, which is difficult to digest, but that is God's way. Genuine love and concern for others builds up our confidence in the Lord. God is the only One that can help us to believe and see that we are somebody. No amount of worldly possessions or prestige can do this. The love of God is what gives men and women their character and allows them to have confidence in a world that focuses solely on self.

High-minded people have the mentality that those who are wealthy are better than those who are not. The Lord commanded that we love all and esteem all equally and above ourselves. James said that if we make a big deal over those that have wealth, we are sinning.

The pseudo-sophisticated make those of lowly means feel worthless with their sharp and piercing words. They know the right buttons to push when it comes to making the less fortunate feel unloved and unwelcome. The damages from their words are like fireballs that shoot straight through the heart.

Humble and meek-hearted people lift up one another with kind words. They are to repair broken hearts and help those that have been pushed aside by busybodies to reclaim their confidence and identity. We should not make people feel uncomfortable with our dirty looks and ugly words.

At some point in our lives, all of us will have people talk about us and lie about us, and our reputations will be damaged to one degree or another. We must not forget who we are in the midst of the falsity. Talk is cheap. We should use the lies of our enemies as fuel for our spiritual growth in Christ. If we turn our bruised egos over to Him, then the negative gossip that is spread about us will not cause us to isolate ourselves from others. We must understand that the lies will continue to surface as long as we live. It is up to us as to how we allow them to shape and form our lives.

The image staring back at you in the mirror does not define who you are as a person. You are a royal priesthood, holy and beautiful, created by the best artist. God used His best clay when He sculpted you, even with all your humanly flaws. He never makes mistakes. You may have a deformity of some kind, you may be paralyzed, you may have a speech impediment, or you may not look the way people want you to look. Undoubtedly, God made you perfect in Him. You need to see yourself as He sees you.

When you look at your reflection in your spiritual mirror, which is the Word of God, you must acknowledge that you have flaws. When you refuse to apply God's law to your mirror image, the spirit of superiority will begin to surface. If you walk away from your spiritual mirror, you will forget the blemishes that it revealed in your own life, and you may begin looking at others' imperfections. God wants you to take a closer look at yourself, so that you can fix all that needs to be changed within you. If you can remember your own reflection and do what needs to be corrected on the inside of you, you will not be so quick to judge or point out the flaws of others.

For if a person just listens and doesn't obey, he is like a man looking at his face in the mirror; as soon as he walks away, he can't see himself anymore or remember what he looks like. But if anyone keeps looking steadily into God's law for free men, he will not only remember it but he will do what it says, and God will greatly bless him in everything he does (James 1:23-25 TLB).

Depending on God

What are you going to do when the damages of the tongue take affect? The love that you once had for yourself will dwindle away without Christ. If you rely solely on the words of others to make you feel happy, motivated, and secure, you are in for a shocker. Only the spirit of God can make a person love what is on the inside of them. No self-help manuals, magazines articles, or makeover shows can do this for you. The power comes from within, and that power is in Jesus Christ alone.

Even if you have been talked about, put down, and discriminated against, never give another human being power over you. Giving them the authority over your life is like telling them that you are inferior and they are superior. Build up your spirit man and confidence in the Lord. Only He has the power to take a person that was almost suicidal and had given up on life and provide a new start to live again. Jude encouraged people to edify themselves in the Lord, knowing that this would be the antidote that would undo the damages of the tongue.

But ye, beloved, building up yourselves on your most holy faith, praying in the Holy Ghost (Jude 1:20 KJV).

Do not sell yourself short. Good things do come from so-called ugly packages; just look at Jesus. The Bible does not describe Him as a handsome man. Consequently, people had difficulty accepting Him as their Savior.

For he shall grow up before him as a tender plant, and as a root out of dry ground; he hath no form nor comeliness; and when we shall see him, there is no beauty that we should desire him (Isaiah 53:2-3 KJV).

The people were looking for a King that was easy on the eyes, tall in stature, educated, well-groomed, and had come from a prominent family. When Jesus did not fit their profile of the King that would rule Israel, they lied about Him, beat Him, rejected Him, and killed Him. Jesus is the best unattractive, beautiful gift ever known to mankind. With all the shame and humiliation that our Savior had to endure, He only held His head down once—not because of what people had said or done to Him, but so He could die that we might live. Hold your head up high, knowing that God has created and packaged something beautiful on the inside of you just waiting to be unwrapped.

Can you imagine how you would feel if you were spat on and beaten because of who you are? Could you have endured this pain as Jesus did? The Bible never says once that He wanted to kill himself or take some type of medication to help cope with such ill treatment. The moment a person does not fit into the world's ideal of beauty and intellect, some men and women want to end it all. But, know that there are those who rose above the damages of the tongue because they believed the Word of the Lord.

- You can do all things in Christ Jesus.
- You are more than a conquer.
- You are the head and not the tale.

Jesus never used the words self-esteem or self-love when referring to Himself. His security and completeness came from the Lord and so should yours.

Let nothing be done through strife or vainglory; but in lowliness of mind let each esteem other better than themselves. Look not every man on his own things, but every man also on the things of others. Let this mind be in you, which was also in Christ Jesus: Who, being in the form of God, thought it not robbery to be equal with God: But made himself of no reputation, and took upon him the form of a servant, and was made in the likeness of men: And being found in fashion as a man, he humbled himself, and became obedient unto death, even the death of the cross (Philippians 2:3-8 KJV).

Satan is the culprit behind our evil words. He shows us a false image of what is attractive, and sadly, we fall for it. He knows that if he can get us confused as to who we are, then he can work his evil plans to destroy us. He works through places such as magazines and television, because they show images of how we are supposed to look, feel, and be. When we do not fit into these categories, we can become depressed. The best sculptor and designer made us wonderful and unique. God put His special touches on us when He carved the clay that would eventually turn into the most beautiful creature that has ever walked this planet—man.

God's Word says in Romans 8:37 that you are more than a conqueror. Use your tongue to speak victory into your life because God has given you the power to take charge over the damages of the tongue. Use your mouthpiece to speak blessings into your life as well as the lives of others. My prayer is that you continue to stand when the fiery darts of the tongue continue to shoot at you because with God you are more than capable to withstand whatever comes your way.

Chapter Four

The Grasshopper Image

And Caleb stilled the people before Moses, and said, Let us go up at once, and possess it; for we are well able to overcome it. But the men that went up with him said, we be not able to go up against the people; for they are stronger than we. And they brought up an evil report of the land which they had searched unto the children of Israel, saying, The land, through which we have gone to search it, is a land that eateth up the habitants thereof; and all the people that we saw in it are men of great stature. And there we saw the giants, the sons of Anak, which come of the giants: and we were in our own sight as grasshoppers, and so we were in their sight (Numbers 13:30-33 KJV).

Do you see yourself as average when compared to others? Do you listen to or believe the negative comments that are said about you? Do you use your weaknesses as a crutch for not doing what God says you can? Do you feel small or inadequate in your own sight? If so, then you are suffering from the grasshopper image.

The grasshopper image is when you magnify someone else's abilities to seem more important or powerful than yours and begin to see yourself as small, inadequate, inferior, and incompetent in comparison. The ten spies in the verses above suffered from the grasshopper image. They concentrated more on their enemies' strength and size instead of remembering how mighty their God was when He fought for them in past battles.

When they called themselves grasshoppers, they doubted who they were as a nation. A grasshopper is an insect that is so small that it can be crushed easily underneath one's feet. That is how the ten spies saw themselves—as nothing—as small insects that could be trampled over at a moment's notice.

They were powerless within themselves, but their God was mighty. The battle was already won. God wanted them to step out in faith and believe that they could occupy the land of prosperity, the land that He had promised so long ago to Abraham and his descendents. The problem began when they started focusing on their adversaries and stopped listening to what God had spoken to them about possessing the land.

Our attitudes mimic those of the children of Israel when God speaks to us to go out and conquer positions on our jobs or step out in faith and start a new career in order to be prosperous. We often make excuses why we can't. We either are scared we might fail or afraid of what people might say or think about us running our own business. Therefore, our pursuits are doomed due to our negative images and lack of faith in what God said we could have.

The problem starts with self. We blame others for our lack of confidence or motivation when tackling tough situations in our lives. The ten spies made every excuse as to why they could not defeat the Canaanites. The men were giants, the people were stronger, and the cities had walls that were too large to climb. They also complained about how their enemies were all around the region. The Amalekites dwelled in the south; the Hittites, Jebusites, Amorites all dwelled in the mountains; and the Canaanites lived by the sea. So, in their minds, the ten spies probably thought that either way they came into Canaan one of these tribes would surely overtake them.

If only the ten spies would have thought about what they were saying. They would have realized that fear of others only held them hostage within their own minds. What we speak is what we have. Breaking free from a negative spirit is difficult when doubting what God has said. He said, "You can do it," but your mind has told you that you can't. Whose report will you believe—God's or man's?

You may feel inferior because of what has been programmed in you by others or by what you have seen. The ten spies became grasshoppers in their own eyes because of what they saw. They saw no breach in their enemies' fortress that would have allowed them to plan a sneak attack. Their men looked like giants, which they thought could have stomped them to death.

The spies had no confidence in their own abilities to conquer the land of Canaan. To make matters worse, they brought their negative reports to Moses and the children of Israel about the people that dwelled in the land. Immediately, their spirits fell. Fear encompassed them, and they felt defeated before the battle began.

Fear has a way of spreading like wildfire. Moses, Joshua, and Caleb had faith in God. The stories of the ten spies were the same; therefore, the people swayed towards their reports. The danger in listening to negative people is that it will keep one living in fear; when this fear is passed on to others, chaos is triggered

If only the Israelites would have had faith, they would have known that there was no battle or anyone tough enough that their God could not subdue. In their eyes, they felt weak compared to the strength that they saw in their enemies. The children of Israel were not aware of the tricks of the devil and did not know that our physical eyes can be deceiving at times. Fear magnifies situations in our lives, and it makes people—in our sight— appear stronger than what they really are. That is why we cannot look at self when it comes to conquering battles against those that have a stronger looking psyche than ours. Battles are not won by strength alone; they are won by strategically outwitting the opponent.

The Israelites are a lot like us. We give up before we try. We complain and blame others for the battles we experience. We allow Satan to get us right where he wants us, with a negative self-image of ourselves. The spirits of inferiority, low self-esteem, inadequacy, and the grasshopper image are all mental weapons of his. They are different words, but their effects are equally devastating, because he uses them to keep us defeated and depressed within our minds. Satan does not want us to move forward in the promises of God. So, he plays on our fears and weakness to keep us trapped with a negative self-image.

No one is immune to this spiritual illness called the grasshopper image. It was designed by Satan to keep God's children in Egypt, which amounts to mental slavery. His job is to cast fear and doubt into the hearts and minds of men. The Bible says, *"For God hath not given us the spirit of fear; but of power, and of love, and of a sound mind"* (2 Timothy 1:7 KJV). So, if our minds are sound, why are we falling apart every time the wind blows? If our minds are powerful, then why can't we see ourselves victorious over the obstacles that cause us to stumble in defeat? And if we have love, why is it

difficult for us to love ourselves enough to know that we are not grasshoppers but spiritual giants over our problems?

If you believe yourself to be nothing, then that is the way people are
going to perceive you to be. Believe it or not, people can sense your lack of
confidence, and when they do, they prey on your weaknesses. You see it all
the time on the reality television shows. If an opponent senses someone's
lack o   l play on the other
person

Th   em out to spy on the
land. I   ord, they would have
known   rd they could defeat
anyon   first starts within the
mind-   es saw themselves as
grassh   inds.

P   s or that in their lives.
But v   rust Him to do what
they   ne fearful. The worst
thing   brought their fear into
their   in Canaan. The spies
pollu   ports and made them
want

When a person is always negative, seeing the bright side to anything in
his or her life is a challenge, and being around people like this will hold you
back. The ten spies did just that with their evil report. The Israelites should
have known that if they had returned to Egypt, they would have been
mocked and forced to resume their positions as slaves. The Egyptians
would have thought that their God had brought them out of Egypt only to
forsake them in the wilderness. Fear and doubt make you believe that you
had it good on the other side of the river, which represents poverty and defeat, when in reality it was a living hell from which only God could have
rescued you. He wants to bring you into a land that is flowing with milk
and honey, which represents prosperity. God will show us the promise and
tell us that He will be with us to bring the promise to pass.

Too often we find that we are fighting a losing battle because we are
afraid of what people will think about us. We allow what people say and
think to keep us from being blessed of the Lord. Sometimes, we think that
we are not worthy of having better, and then we allow Satan to rob us of

our blessings. He wants us to believe that we are not capable of having a better life. Therefore, we stay in the land of poverty because of the negative image we have of ourselves.

Defeating the Giants

God can take the smallest of things to defeat those that are of great stature. When King David was a boy, he defeated and killed one of the greatest giants of his day—Goliath. Goliath challenged Saul and his army in a single dual, but they were afraid to fight him one-on-one because he stood nine feet tall. David accepted the challenge to defeat Goliath, and he told King Saul, *"The Lord that delivered me out of the paw of the lion, and out of the paw of the bear, he will deliver me out of the hand of the Philistine"* (1 Samuel 17:37 KJV). When David stood in battle with Goliath, the giant looked at David with contempt; little did he know that David had the Lord on his side. *"Then said David to the Philistine, Thou comest to me with a sword, and with a spear, and with a shield: but I come to thee in the name of the Lord of hosts, the God of the armies of Israel, whom thou hast defied"* (1 Samuel 17:45 KJV). David took one of his smooth stones, put it in a sling, and hit Goliath in the forehead. The giant fell to the ground, and David took Goliath's sword and finished the job. The old saying goes, "The bigger they are, the harder they fall."

If only the children of Israel had faith in what David believed when they came face to face with the giants of Anak, they would have been in the Promised Land in a matter of days instead of forty years. They too should have spoken like David when he said that the Lord would deliver him out of his enemies' hands. They saw how God parted the Red Sea and kept their enemies at bay with a fire while waiting for it to dry before crossing to the other side to freedom. How could their faith have weakened so soon?

Are we that much different when facing the giants in our lives? Fear is the giant that is often governing our lives. If we let it go unchecked, it will keep us from growing and blossoming into the person that God has called us to be. We are allowing negative conversations about us from others to stunt our growth. We worry about what people say and think about us more than what God thinks or says. We have allowed their lies to emotionally stagnant us. We lack confidence in God, as well as ourselves, because of how we perceive ourselves to be physically and spiritually. We believe that we are failures. Why? Because it has been planted in our heads by others that are trying to make us feel ashamed of our heritage and who we are. These are the spiritual giants that we are faced with every day.

Defeating the Workplace Giants

The grasshopper image is also found on our jobs. Whether it exists through our coworkers or us, the spirit of inferiority does not discriminate. People are willing to be mistreated and abused by their employers and coworkers in order to climb up the corporate ladder to achieve vain success. All one has to do is just look around one's work environment and see people that are willing to compromise their dignity in order to be a part of the "in" crowd. We hate being belittled but are too afraid to speak out against it for fear that we will be shunned by coworkers or fired. We allow people to walk all over us because of the need to be accepted.

Success is a state of mind, not how fast and hard you play to move up the corporate ladder. Stepping on others and making them feel useless is not the way it should be done. Many coworkers can be ruthless and conniving in their approach to others. You must be willing to stand against their intimidation and sarcasm towards you. Seek God before approaching situations like these. He will show you how to handle combative coworkers without being fearful.

I have witnessed in my own experiences on numerous jobs that when people are hurting, they will try to make you feel the same way. Keep in mind that people bring a lot of baggage from home and dump it at the job. They want to hurt you because that is how they are feeling inside. It is not that you have done anything to provoke their behavior. Before you harbor their injustice towards you in your heart, pray. Most people take it personally and never get over the pain of an abusive boss or coworker, but you must do so before the grasshopper image consumes you and strips you of your identity.

Now more than ever, people are using their sick leave because of work related stress. They have fallen into the grasshopper image. If they had confidence in themselves, they would know that God did not create them to be doormats. You do not have to let people walk all over you because of the positions or titles that they hold in the workplace. You deserve to be respected. Some people in society are prominent and influential, but that does not give them the right to treat others as any less.

Many people cannot handle power. People like this make the worst bosses or supervisors. They use their authority to mistreat their employees. They do so because of the underlining insecurities of their own abilities to do the job. Often they have scratched and clawed to get their positions without any qualifications. Now they are scared that someone with more experience will take their jobs so they set out to make those that work under them feel useless and unimportant. Eventually, the person quits, and they hire an employee with fewer qualifications that will not outshine them.

The grasshopper image is causing people to become emotional wrecks from the time they clock in on the job until the time they clock out. They know that their day will be dreadful due to managers and supervisors that have no awareness of the truth of God. If they really reverenced God and served Him, they would be better at managing and treating their employees with respect.

Evidently many employers aren't watching the news, because if they were, they would see how the mistreatment of their employees is like a volcano waiting to erupt. When bosses cause their employees to feel as though they hold less value than an insect, those employees will take a combative approach to the job and harm everyone in sight—even those that are innocent. Many people who have been stepped on through the years cannot take the pressure of an abusive boss or coworkers anymore and act out aggressively as a result.

In contrast, the workers that know who they are in Christ pray about the injustice of their employers, and they leave it in the hands of Him to handle. They pray when they arrive and pray when they leave. They understand that the power of prayer will keep them in perfect peace. The ugly and belittling words spoken by a supervisor or coworker do not depress or discourage them. They know that when people lack confidence within themselves, they will try to make others feel the same. Being alienated by coworkers is not a problem for them because of the love of God that they have in their hearts. It helps them to cope with the day-to-day attacks. They have no fear of what the day will bring because they have confidence that the Lord will give them the strength to stand.

How do you see yourself? I pray that after reading this chapter, you will see yourself as a giant. Therefore you can face your oppositions head on, knowing that your size does not determine how the battle is going to end; how you see yourself when going into the battle is what drives the outcome. I pray you will see yourself as a warrior that has reclaimed your dignity, self-esteem, and confidence.

Chapter Five

Conquering Your Fears

I remember as if it were yesterday when God spoke to my spirit about writing a book. I did not want to attempt the task because of fear—fear of what others would think when I told them what God was calling me to do. I had to pray long and hard to God just in case I didn't hear Him correctly. When I held the book in my hands for the first time, I thought that I would faint because it was now a reality. The secret that I kept for eight long months was now out in the open. As a first time author three years ago, I had to learn how to conquer my fears against those who knew me best. Would they accept my new calling? Or would they perceive it as a joke? At any rate, I trusted God and overcame my trepidation to be the person that He called me to be. I did not let what others thought of me change the course and path that God had for my life.

If you do not conquer your fears, steps in your life's journey will be delayed. If God told you to step out in faith and believe in His Word, what else do you need? Maybe you have allowed others to tell you what you can and cannot do. Some people do not want to see you move forward in the things of God so they use their negative influences to try and hold you back. Don't be blind to the tricks of the enemy when he comes to poison your mind with self-doubt. As long as those around you can stop you from dreaming of bettering yourself through Christ, they will try every trick in the book to keep you from succeeding and moving forward to a life of prosperity.

Those that pretended to be your friends loved it when you felt defeated and had to lean and depend on their phony support—thinking that they meant you well when they really did not. They gloated over the fact that they had you believing that they were your friends when all along they stuck close to you to make sure that your dreams would never come to fruition. Look, listen, and learn their tricks. Sometimes people stick close to you in the guise of friendship just to keep feeding you negative information in hopes of stagnating your life's plans.

Whenever you talk about the positive things that God is doing in your life, watch their conversation turn negative. With God there is no negativity in what He speaks. God only wants to empower your life through His words. He wants to set you free from the crippling words that have been planted and rooted in your mind by family and so-called friends. God knows that you cannot move forward in Him until you have mentally and spiritually broken that defeated image of yourself. He wants you to see your self-worth in Him so that you will not give others the power to turn your dreams into nightmares.

I was always told from a very young age, "Peace of mind is worth more than money in the bank." You can sleep at night without a care in the world, knowing that God will protect you from the slander of your enemies. Remember that talk is cheap. Never give a person power over you because the moment you do, you will surely be defeated. You cannot choose the family that you were born into, but you can choose your friends and the people that you allow in your life. Even with family members, God can set you free from their abuse as well. You have the choice of not allowing them to strip you of the self-confidence that God has placed within you.

Getting the Right Perspective

Complaining is another action that keeps us from conquering our fears. We complain to the point that we never see the good that God is doing and has done in our lives. In addition to grumbling with our words, we can also have a complaining attitude that can prove to be self-destructive.

My pastor preached a sermon that caught my attention when he said, "You are the worst person that you know." No one can argue with that fact because you know yourself better than anyone else does. No one knows your insecurities and fears the way you do. One of the reasons that you inflict pain on others may be so that you can release the misery that is on the inside of you.

If things are not going right in your life, check your attitude. Are you always bemoaning about your lack of ability? It's time to face your fears and step out in faith and say, "Yes, I can do this with the Lord on my side." Because God said that He would make you victorious over the obstacles in your life, fear should no longer be the factor that controls you.

We gripe because we fail to remember all the battles that the Lord has fought and won for us. Our enemies lie in wait to ambush us with the bitterness of their tongues, but God has guarded our hearts and minds from it. He was there to protect us when they wanted to terrorize us with fear and to keep us believing that we would never amount to anything.

God was the voice that kept speaking to us to let go of past hurts, which should have been the starting point of taking control of our fears. We began to complain and murmur against God because we believed that He did not understand how people have torn us apart with their ugly comments. We began to sulk and wallow in our self-misery until we made our enemies and their words giants in our lives.

I can only imagine how Joshua and Caleb must have felt. They believed in what God had told them, but the others let the alarming reports cause them to doubt not only their abilities but also God's. Where is our faith? Why do we allow people to tell us what we can and cannot do? Is God still in control of our lives? Those are the same questions that Joshua and Caleb had asked. They knew that with God, they could defeat any giant that stood in their way. All the people had to do was believe.

The Israelites were so close to entering the Promised Land, but because of complaining, fear, doubt, and lack of faith, God allowed them to wander in the wilderness. This would torture me mentally, knowing that I was so close to fulfilling God's promises, only to allow fear, complaining, and grumbling to get in the way.

Then all the people began weeping aloud, and they carried on all night. Their voices rose in a great chorus of complaint against Moses and Aaron. "We wish we had died in Egypt," they wailed, "or even here in the wilderness, rather than be taken into this country ahead of us. Jehovah will kill us there, and our wives and little ones will become slaves. Let's get out of here and return to Egypt!" they shouted (Numbers 14:1-4 TLB).

Then the Lord added to Moses and to Aaron, "How long will these wicked people complain about me? For I have heard all that they have been saying. Tell them, 'The Lord vows to do to you what you feared: You will die here in the wilderness! Not a single one of you twenty years old and older, who has complained against me, shall enter the Promised Land. Only Caleb (son of Jephunneh) and Joshua (son of Nun) are permitted to enter it (Numbers 14:26-30 TLB).

Fear is your worst enemy because it causes you to lose faith. When you complain, what you have dreaded the most—failure—begins to become reality. Many people will die in their situations because they cannot see past their "poor is me" attitude.

God told Moses to tell the people that what they feared the most would be the very thing that would destroy them, instead of conquering and living in the land that God had promised and prepared for them—a land that was already fertile. All they had to do was conquer it and move in, but the Israelites would wander in circles in the wilderness until all those that complained against God had died. Fear was the culprit that caused them not to live the life that He had planned for them. Fear can be the force that destroys us today. It becomes a mind struggle when we try to break free from the negative reports of people that seek to keep us terrified.

The devil will always paint the picture to make it seem as though life was good when you were being mentally, physically, and spiritually beaten down by those that had control over you. As soon as God wants to deliver you from those bad situations and take you to a place where you can be free, you rebel. Satan does not want you to know that through Christ there is deliverance from the negative reports that had you bound to the pressures of life. Griping and whining will keep you in those predicaments until you eventually die spiritually and physically.

Victory With the Lord

There is power in small numbers when God is in the midst of them. Forget the saying, "the majority rules." Scripture teaches, *"How should one chase a thousand, and two put ten thousand to flight, except their Rock had sold them, and the Lord had shut them up?"* (Deuteronomy 32:30 KJV). No man can fight a battle alone unless his Rock—the Lord of lords is with him. Only God can stop a mighty war from raging against you. Only He can take that same war and make you victorious with small numbers.

Look at Gideon, for example. He had an army of men that consisted of thirty-two thousand, and God reduced it to only three hundred to fight in the battle against the Midianites. He did this so that Gideon and the people of Israel would know that God had won the battle against their enemies and not the power of man.

No doubt, Gideon probably thought that God was joking when He kept saying that he had too many men in his army, when the Midianites had 135,000. God wanted him to know that power does not come in numbers but through Him. If Gideon had been looking at his problems through his natural eyes, it would have meant defeat. When he looked at his situation through the eyes of God, he believed through faith that he and his men with God were just as mighty as their enemies were.

God wants us to see ourselves as victorious—even if we have to stand alone. True, there is physical power in numbers; but with God, He can turn the strongest of men into weaklings. When God spoke to Gideon about being the one to save Israel, he was unsure of himself. God told him that he would be successful in defeating the Midianites. Gideon said, *"Oh my Lord, wherewith shall I save Israel? behold, my family is poor in Manasseh, and I am the least in my father's house"* (Judges 6:15 KJV).

Most of us feel the same way as Gideon did about our family backgrounds. We have allowed society to tell us what we can and cannot be because of the neighborhoods we came from and our family backgrounds. God can take what men consider to be nothing and make that person to be great in the sight of others. He did this with Gideon, and He can do the same for us.

It's time to rise above the influences of fear and see yourself as the victor in everything that you set out to do. When you have conquered your fears, you can move on to the next chapter of your life. With faith, prayer, and determination, the sky will be the limit for you when you finally believe the report of the Lord.

Chapter Six

Dominating Spirits

David is still one of the most celebrated kings today. God promised him fame beyond his wildest dreams and a destiny that would remain forever. David was a sheepherder from a poor family and was the youngest among his brothers. God saw something in him that the human eye could not see. Although David would sin, God knew his heart.

Now therefore so shalt thou say unto my servant David, Thus saith the Lord of host, I took thee from the sheepcote, from following the sheep, to be ruler over my people, Israel: and I was with thee whithersoever thou wentest, and have cut off all thine enemies out of thy sight, and have made thee a great name, like unto the name of the great men that are in the earth (2 Samuel 7:8-9 KJV).

If God promised to do this for David, surely He will do the same for you. God protected you when you did not know that you were being protected. He is calling you out of your dominating relationships to make your name great above those that called you stupid and worthless. He wants to do this for you no matter what may have happened in your family background. If you have been molested or experienced any other kind of physical or verbal abuse that triggered a subservient persona in your life, God can take it away and make you stand tall before those that have tried to strip you of your dignity.

So what if those that have tried to keep you depressed cannot believe that God can take a fragile flower such as yourself and make something great of you. It is their loss because they will miss out on seeing you grow into the beautiful, strong flower that God has nurtured. They wanted to pluck you before God was finished caring for you, but His loving arms shielded you from their harm. God wants to see to it that you blossom, so that all those that tried to destroy you with their dominating spirits could take notice of how a beautiful rose sprouted from among the thorns and thistles—the enemy's stronghold.

Domination in Marriage

The spirit of domination exists in many marriages, where one partner controls the relationship. One person makes the other partner feel incompetent and dependent upon him or her for support within the union. In some marriages, the woman is the one who feels bossed around, because the male is often the aggressive one in the relationship.

According to Scriptures, God made man the head of his household. With that authority, He also gave him guidelines to follow when it comes to his wife because God never meant for a woman to live in constant fear of her husband:

1. *And you husbands, show the same kind of love to your wives as Christ showed to the church when he died for her, to make her holy and clean, washed by baptism and God's Word; so that he could give her to himself as a glorious church without a single spot or wrinkle or any other blemish, being holy and without a single fault. That is how husbands should treat their wives, loving them as parts of themselves. For since a man and his wife are now one, a man is really doing himself a favor and loving himself when he loves his wife!* (Ephesians 5:25-28 TLB).

2. *And you husbands must be loving and kind to your wives and not bitter against them, nor harsh* (Colossians 3:19 TLB).

Times have drastically changed from the Bible days. Now some men deal with living in fear of their wives. This statement might sound comical because a man appears to be stronger physically than a woman, but most of them are dealing with what women have gone through for centuries. They also suffer from the spirit of domination within their marriages. If you just look at your married friends or yourself if you are married, you can tell which of the two dominates the relationship.

God never meant for you to be in fear or feel inferior within the relationships that He has ordained. Within your marriage, God wants you to be free and not enslaved, never having to walk on eggshells when you are around your mate.

Although many are not being physically abused in their marriages, verbal abuse is just as deadly and toxic. It causes men or women to be self-conscious of everything they do. It isolates them from others, because they do not feel worthy of being treated fairly or loved. The fear factor will cause them to spiral into a state of depression if they cannot break free from the chains of verbal abuse.

Many people accept a marriage relationship that includes verbal abuse because they are fearful of what will happen to them if they left their abusive spouses. They wonder who would love and take care of them if they decided to leave. If only they would realize that love does not hurt, or insult, or destroy; instead, love comforts, compliments, and builds.

Bullies and Children

In our schools today, our kids are suffering from being bullied because they do not fit in with the so-called "in crowd." They are not allowed to be creative or to be themselves. When they do not measure up to the other kids' standards of what is popular and acceptable, their peers tease and taunt them as if something is mentally or physically wrong with them. This is one of the reasons why we may have school shootings and kids committing crimes at an alarming rate in our schools and neighborhoods.

It seems as though no one is paying attention to the problem until it is too late. After these kids take the schools under siege, everyone wants to know what went wrong. The problem is that we did not pay attention to the warning signs. We saw the behaviorial changes in our children but never stopped to investigate until it was too late. We never asked why they were afraid to go to school. We did not know that they were being bullied until that fateful day the child decided to take a gun to school for protection.

Fear is dangerous when help is not sought for problems. If a person is made to feel like nothing and is picked on incessantly, fear will cause that person to do unthinkable things that he or she never considered before. We need to talk with our children and encourage them. Let them know that they are important and that kids only pick and tease on them because they are insecure themselves. If the problem persists, we need to seek help because our children are not spiritually or mentally mature enough to handle tough situations such as these. That is why they are making deadly choices. Being laughed at and stepped on are not only destructive to our children, but also to others that may cross their paths.

A poor self-image can be potentially dangerous or fatal if the person does not know who he or she is in Christ. To them, they see themselves as misfits, not worthy to exist in this society so they feel no remorse if they take their lives as well as others. The healing process of an unhealthy image can begin to mend when we search the Scriptures and allow God through His Holy Word to show us who He says we are.

1. We are the light that cannot be hidden. (No matter how people may try to dim it, God's love for us keeps it shining brightly.)
2. We are the salt of the earth. (Salt takes over whatever it is sprinkled over and so should we.)
3. We are His masterpiece. (He is the potter and we are the clay.)

Hindrances to Growth

Dominating spirits are hindrances to your spiritual growth. You will never know what you can or cannot do unless you step out of your shell. You must dig deep inside yourself and overcome every negative thing that has happened to you. Most people cannot let go of bad childhood memories because they tucked those demons deep inside their hearts. As adults, they are still holding on to those images of bullies that tortured and terrorized them in school. You must let go in order for you to grow.

On many talk shows, guests appear that cannot get past being talked about and bullied at a young age. When they recount what happen to them to the audience, they sob so uncontrollably that one would think the offense recently happened. These people still live their lives in the past. Their bullies do not know, in most cases, that the person is still affected by what they did or said years before. To them, it was just childhood teasing; but to their victims, it made them develop an inferiority complex.

Let us not stand accused of asserting ourselves over others. We are to show love and compassion to those that cannot get over their traumatic pasts. We are to help them understand that thinking less of themselves is a stronghold that will prevent them from becoming the people that God has created them to be.

If you allow others to control the way you think, feel, and act, they will keep you from moving forward in your life. The devil knows this, which is why he does not want others that have been delivered from his stronghold to tell you how they broke free from this debilitating sickness. The power is within you. Find the door that will set your mind free from thinking too little of yourself. This door leads to spiritual freedom and will allow you to see yourself as conquering those dominating spirits that have tried to keep you bound.

Today is a new day in your life. It's time to take charge and stop allowing others to dominate you or to put you in an inferior position. Stop putting yourself in situations that cause you to be walked on like a doormat. You deserve to be loved, respected, and adored; it's time that you realize this and take a stand against any dominating spirits in your life.

Chapter Seven

Partiality

Now as it happened, Israel loved Joseph more than any of his other chil-
dren, because Joseph was born to him in his old age. So one day Jacob
gave him a special gift—a brightly-colored coat. His brothers of course
noticed their father's partiality, and consequently hated Joseph; they
couldn't say a kind word to him (Genesis 37:3-4 TLB).

Partiality towards our children is just as dangerous as handing them a
loaded gun and telling them to pull the trigger. It will eventually take its
toll on them. We as parents are sending the wrong message that it's okay to
favor one child over the other. At times, we forget that kids are like ticking
time bombs that will sooner or later explode. Kids and young adults are
committing many violent crimes in America. They do not know how to
handle rejection, especially rejection from a parent. Unfortunately, they
sometimes respond in ways that are deadly to themselves and others.

Look at what our children have become. They are a generation that is
estranged from their biological siblings. In some cases, the problem stems
back to childhood. They do not know how to show affection because they
did not receive or feel it as a child. In essence, they become angry adults
that unleash their frustrations and pain onto their siblings and others. They
are hurting and want others to feel the same. Through their loneliness,
feelings of being unloved and unwanted, bullies are formed, serial killers are
born, and spouse abusers are created. They may become teens and young
adults that suffer with low self-esteem and a poor self-image. It may cause
them to become withdrawn from others as well. In their minds, they believe that if their mothers or fathers do not love them, then no one else

will. The mind can only take so much before it injects its deadly poison into others—with often violent consequences.

On the other hand, not all kids take what happened to them in their childhoods to the extreme of harming others or themselves. Many will rise above what took place as they grew up and become over achievers, trying to earn their parents' love and respect. They feel that success will make them stand out in the eyes of their parents. And they will spend a lifetime trying to receive their parents' approval. They take these extreme routes because of two little words—love and acceptance.

Jacob's Mistakes

Jacob, who is also known as Israel, put himself in the same position that many parents are in today—he favored one of his children over the others. Jacob loved his son Joseph more because he was conceived in Jacob's old age. Although Jacob had two wives, Leah and Rachael, he showed his love and affection towards Joseph's mother, Rachael. Jacob should have known from his past that being partial toward siblings would only lead to trouble in the end.

Although we know that Jacob's story has a happy ending with his children, we can still learn lessons from his mistakes. We know that it was in God's divine plan for Jacob's family and the nation of Israel to survive (see Genesis 37-46). Partiality and its dangers are best learned when we do not follow the poor parenting skills of others that will drive a wedge between siblings. If we fail to learn, history will repeat itself.

The guilt and the shame that Joseph's brothers had to live with for years (selling their brother as a slave and faking his death) could have easily been avoided if their father had treated each of his children equally. Jacob was forced to live with the thought that wild animals had eaten his beloved Joseph.

Joseph's brothers hated him because he was a tattletale. When he saw his brothers up to mischief, he snitched on them to his father. Strike one. To make matters worse, he flaunted his coat of many colors that his father had given to him as a gift. Strike two. God blessed Joseph to see into the future. In his dreams, God revealed to him that his brothers and father would be kneeling before him and that he would rule over them. He told these dreams to his brothers, and they became so bitter towards him that they couldn't speak a civil word to him. Strike three.

Joseph reminds me of our children today. When they think that their parents have given them something that their siblings do not have, they cannot wait to brag about it. They know when they are receiving special treatment from their parents. Even before a baby can talk or walk, the infant knows when he or she is being favored and spoiled. They will kick, cry, and fight when someone tries to move into their territory. Joseph's brothers must have felt the same way. Children don't want to believe that their parents prefer their brother or sister to them.

Children Are a Gift

What makes one child more deserving of our love than the other? It is not right to love and favor the child that excels in school more than the one that is barely making the grade or esteem one over the other due to his or her attractiveness. The love of a parent should not come with conditions. No kids are the same. They all have different gifts, talents, and abilities, which make them unique. Our home would be a boring place to live if each of our children was exactly the same.

Low self-esteem, depression, and early usage of drugs and alcohol in kids may stem from them not being accepted by their parents. Sadly children in our society are facing this dilemma in their homes each day: parents bestow love on one child, while ignoring the other child as one would a stranger on the streets. It's hard enough that low self-esteem is a typical part of the adolescent stage of growing up, but rejection from the parent only makes this difficult season worse. When peer pressure is added into the equation, more fuel is added to the flames of uncertainty.

If God made us unique, and He loves us whether we fail or succeed, then why are we as parents tough on our kids when they do not achieve the goals that we have set for them? Does that make them any less our children? If they do not live up to our expectations, will we love the one that has succeeded and followed our plans for his or her life more than the one who hasn't?

We cannot totally blame society, television, and magazines for the misbehavior of our children. As parents, we can only blame ourselves for creating a generation of confused children. We have created the rift that separates our kids from one another. The child that is singled out as the failure or black sheep of the family may grow into an adult with issues stemming back to his or her childhood. And the pattern will continue until the child can see and feel the love that you should have shown them in his or her youth. It is hard for that individual to show love if it has never been a part of that person's upbringing. But, with God, it's never too late for this to be learned, because He set the greatest example of how to love.

Can you imagine having a brother or sister that you have no dealings with as an adult because of what transpired in your childhood? Many people cannot let go of the hurt that they experienced as a child, and it will manifest itself into their adult lives when they become parents. How can you give or show love when you do not know how to love? Love is taught first by the parents and passed on to the child. Because a parent's love runs deep, belittling from a parent is the worst kind of rejection.

Just talk to children that grew up in abusive homes. No matter how their parents may have hurt them, they still have love in their hearts. Yes, it hurts them deeply, but they have hope that they can do something to make their parents happy or proud of them so the abuse will stop. The children have to learn that the problem is not with them; it is with the parents. The parents have unresolved issues within themselves that are being released onto the child. But, children will do whatever it takes to earn their parents' love and affection no matter how bad it may hurt.

Children are a gift from God. Jesus will hold those accountable that mistreat them. He says, *"But if any of you causes one of these little ones who trust in me to lose his faith, it would be better for you to have a rock tied to your neck and be thrown into the sea"* (Matthew 18:6 TLB). God placed the innocence of children in the hands of the parents to protect and nurture them as they grow in Christ. Those that have taken away their innocence and safety will have to answer to Him. There is never room for partiality with the Savior, because He never made any differences or comparison between us—He is not a respecter of persons.

Our children will attach themselves to people that make them feel loved, especially young girls. Whether it is the father or a stranger on the street, they will go where they can find love—superficial or real. Psychologists have researched that young women are attractive to men that are like their fathers. But, what if that father is verbally or physically abusive?

The first person to either destroy or validate a young girl's self-worth is her father. He is the first man in her life to tell her how beautiful and smart she is. He is the one that encourages her to follow her dreams and tells her that she can do anything that she sets her mind to do. But if that father is the type of man that does not respect women, the daughter, as she grows older, will believe that this type of behavior expresses the way real love should be.

Girls often attach themselves to the first boy or man that tells them that they are pretty because they never heard it as a child from their fathers. They feel insincere in who they are and will accept any compliment no matter who says it. In some cases, the boy or man will use and abuse her as a form of control. She accepts it because she was not taught by her father to be confident. A man can sense a woman's insecurities a mile away. He will prey on her lack of self-esteem with verbal or physical abuse until he makes her believe that she is worthless. This is especially true if that is what she has heard all of her life. This will reinforce in her mind that what her father said is true: "You are ugly, and no one will ever love you."

Fathers, your daughters need you now in these days more than ever. Your child is living in a world full of predators just waiting to destroy their self-worth and take their lives. You will be responsible for sending them right into their hands if you are not showing them love. They need to have confidence in you. A girl's first love is her daddy. In you, she will learn the difference between a good man and a bad one. You will teach her how to see herself through the eyes of God, as well as through the eyes of a loving father. Your daughter will learn how to give love because you have shown her first how to love—the right way.

Mothers, teach your boys that it's all right to cry and to show their emotions. Stop calling them sissies because they want to express their feelings. Know that a real boy or man will reveal his innermost thoughts and feelings. Stop comparing him to his deadbeat father (if that's what he is) every time he does something you dislike. When he receives sarcastic name calling as a youth, it sinks into his mind; he may eventually become what is said about him. You are creating a problem for his future wife. Speak positive comments about him. Let him know how proud you are of him, whether he plays football or takes dance lessons.

If we as parents would just stop and think about our actions and the hurtful words that we sometimes speak to our children, we would realize the long-term effects that they can have on them. Words cut like a knife, especially to our kids who are so vulnerable and impressionable. Their adolescence years are the most sensitive time of their lives. Everybody wants to be loved—even an animal acts up when it is not loved. When a child sees that you love his or her siblings more than him or her, rebellion may result; it does not take a psychologist to predict this. Some parents know that they are causing a rift between their children but do not care to repair the damages. In their minds, they believe their children will grow out of it, but millions do not.

A child, no matter how cruel he or she has been treated by a parent, will believe that he or she can do something to please or make that parent proud—if only for a moment. As an adult, that person still has an ambition that if only he or she can be the son or daughter that the parent always wanted, maybe love and affection from the parent can be earned. For many adult children, that day will never come because change has to start with the parent. The problem lies within the parent, not with the child. Some parents will never see and appreciate the gifts that God has blessed them with—even when they are staring them in the face. They see their children as pieces of temporary property and treat them as such.

It's heartbreaking to believe that parents can show partiality to a child that they have birthed into the world. Some people are not cut out to be parents. A real parent loves and nurtures each child, not just the one that does everything just the way the parent likes it. Mothers and fathers seem to forget that children understand more than they think. Children know when they are treated differently than their siblings. You can see it in their behavior.

I can remember when my two girls were babies; both would make sure that I would not spend too much time with the other. As I look back at videotapes, both are making sure that they get equal camera time. Kids are smart, and they recognize when you are neglecting them. They will cry, act up, and rebel to get your attention. Our children are rebelling today. Many of them are not bad kids; they do bad things sometimes to get their parents' attention.

Our kids are acting up at school because of what is taking place in their homes. We take them to doctors that prescribe behavioral medications, thinking that this will solve the problem. The medicines only turn them into zombies and create an even bigger problem. (I am not making light of the many kids that really need to take behavioral medication.) What our children need is love. We spend so much time avoiding them that we do not know what is going on in their little minds. The only prescription that many of them need is love and attention from their parents; no medication can provide this.

Parents, wake up and pay attention to the signs. Despite what you think, society is not the first to influence our children. Whatever takes place inside our homes impacts our children first, whether positive or negative. Stop judging your son's masculinity on whether he plays sports or your daughter's beauty solely on her outward appearance. They are crying out more than ever for their parents' love and attention. It's time to hear those cries before it is too late.

How would you feel if God compared you to someone else? What if He treated him or her as more special than you? Would you like it? How would it affect your level of confidence? Would it make you act out and rebel? Then, just think for a moment about how your actions towards each of your children makes them feel.

Partiality within many of our homes is real. But parents, with God it's never too late to rectify this problem. There is no greater love to a child than the love of a parent. If you are dealing with issues of the past that's keeping you from giving parental love and affection to your child, seek help. Because each child needs you emotionally and spiritually, when you connect with them on this level, the pain of partiality will no longer be an issue in their lives.

Chapter Eight

The Rift Between Siblings

Jacob's problems began when he was a young man. He stole his brother Esau's birthright. In the Bible days, the eldest male child inherited all his father's riches when he died. Jacob dressed himself in his brother's clothes so that their father would think that he was Esau. At that time, Isaac was old and his vision was dim, so it was easy to trick him.

The lies and deceit caused friction between the two brothers, which caused them to become alienated from one another. In his old age, Jacob caused the same spirit of competitiveness to enter into his home once again. Although we know the outcome to this story, it still does not justify Jacob treating one child better than the others.

Showing preferences among your children sends mixed messages. They may develop resentment, anger, and a violent behavior towards the one who is treated in a special way. I can only imagine the hurt and pain Jacob's other boys must have felt, knowing that their father could have so much love for one child. Wasn't there enough love to go around? Sibling rivalry resulted in Joseph's brothers plot to kill him, which proves that you cannot be partial with your love because it may cause the other children to retaliate—in some cases violently.

We need to realize that not every family will have a Joseph that will repair the family. Many times the rift cannot be mended; some people are destroyed forever because of what transpired in their childhoods. Once the children grow up and move out of the home, they never return because of the emotional damage and baggage that they are still carrying around from their youth. They are scarred for life—and to think, it was by the hands that had given them life.

Emphasizing Appearances

A rift can arrive in families that place more emphasis on their children's outer appearances than what is on the inside. Parents may expect their children (especially girls) to be beautiful, thin, and flawless. If one of the children fails to meet their parents' standard of beauty, they become the butt of the family jokes. Children comparing themselves to their more attractive siblings is one thing, but hearing judgments from their mother or father makes the hurt even worse.

Society has become addicted to the skeleton look, and our children are killing themselves to make their bodies conform to that image. As parents, we can make matters worse for our children when they are already going through the identity crisis period in their lives. To criticize them for being overweight and less attractive does not make it easier for them. We should be teaching our children that they are beautiful no matter what size or shape they are. Mothers have a responsibility not to cause the seed that grew inside of them for nine months to suffer pain and humiliation by their words and actions to the point that our children wish that they had never been born.

The television show, *Celebrity Fit Club*, had one of its stars confess that his mother had emotionally damaged him by referring to him as the "fat twin." She made all types of negative remarks concerning his weight. She consistently compared him to his brother, who was smaller than he was. Therefore, he dieted and had plastic surgery to tighten those areas on his body that he thought retained fat. He was not overweight. He was the right size and height for a man his age, but the emotional scars from his childhood led him to believe differently. Words from your parents have long-lasting effects and some are so deep rooted, no matter how people may tell you that there is nothing wrong with you, still you have trouble believing them. Any verbal abuse and ridicule that you received from your parents in your early years has influenced you.

Parents sometimes boast to others that they gave their kids everything in their childhood. When they become adults, they will tell you that they grew up lonely and starved for love and affection from their parents. It may appear that they gave their child the best that life had to offer, when in reality they are the best that life has to offer in a child's life. Yes, kids like toys and gifts, but toys and gifts without you causes your love to mean nothing to them.

Preferences and discrimination in many black families and communities are a reality. Having existed for years, this truth is rarely mentioned. Adult children that have suffered from these acts are still feeling the stigma from it and can attest to these truths.

I have witnessed where the lighter children in black families are treated better than the rest. The parents make the darker skinned children feel that they are ugly and dumb. To make matters worse, usually the mother is the one that shows a preference between her children in situations such as these. The darker child is made to feel that he or she has been cursed because they do not look like everyone else in the family. This individual is also made to feel that he or she is no good, untrustworthy, and sneaky. When the light skinned child sees the mother's favoritism with the lighter children, they mimic the mother's behavior.

Racism and stereotypes exist within black families, and we distinguish each other by the color of our skin as well. We are allowing our kids to grow up feeling ashamed of being dark skinned. It was once taught that it is a curse to be black. This lie has been passed down to our young and beautiful black children. This myth was taken out of context with Ham's son Canaan and his descendants when Noah cursed them to be the lowest of slaves to the descendents of his brothers, Japheth and Shem (see Genesis 9-10). God knew the colors He wanted each race to be even before the earth was formed.

The Tara Banks Show aired an episode where one of the guests from Africa said, "If a girl has a dark complexion, the light skinned men would rape her, so that their children would be a lighter complexion." What does this message sends to a young girl's self-esteem? This is one of the worst forms of making a child feel lower than an animal, because this tells her that she does not matter. She is made to feel that the color of her skin is not acceptable in this society.

Although we know that God created all things beautiful, we in the black community destroy our young boys and girls by making them feel inferior because of their dark complexion. It makes no difference to be light skinned if your heart is as black as coal. As a people of multiple colors and shades, we should embrace our children's differences and teach them to love the skin that they are in. God thought enough of us to make us unique. He does not look at the color of a person's skin but at the heart.

On the sitcom, *Girlfriends,* the character Tony Childs proved my point that many blacks discriminate towards one another. She wanted to meet a guy that was rich on an online dating service. Well, she got her wish—he was rich—but when she met him, he was also dark skinned, which immediately was a turnoff for her. She did not want a man that was dark, no matter how much money he made. She feared that if she married someone that had a dark complexion and she was also dark, then the child would be even darker. She believed that if they had a child, he or she would be teased and ridiculed. She said kids called her, "Big Lips" and "Skillet" because she was dark skinned. They also joked about her nappy hair. She refused to have a child of hers face the same torture.

This is the message that is being passed down to many of our black youths by their parents: if you are not light skinned, you are not beautiful. Does skin complexion define beauty? It's bad enough when you see it on television, when black actresses (who feel the pressure more than black male actors) are cast in movies and videos. Most of them are light skinned or can pass for white, which reinforces the sting of being singled out because of the shade of your skin.

Patti LaBelle (famed R&B and Gospel singer) was told that she was too black and ugly to make it as a singer. Her voice was beautiful, but that did not matter to those pulling the strings in the entertainment business. Good thing that she did not listen because she is one of the most recognizable and talented singers of our day. She believed enough in herself not to listen to those that wanted to define her beauty by the complexion of her skin. She had to face those that wanted to be partial against her. She defied the odds and broke the stigma that her black skin was ugly compared to other lighter skinned black singers (whose talents were no match for hers).

Subjectivity exists in all races, not just in black communities. Every race has parents that show favoritism towards one of their children. In the parent's ignorance, this holier-than-thou attitude gets passed on to the child, which in turn makes that individual believe that he or she is superior to a sibling. This child will become the real victim, because this behavior will be passed on to his or her children unless the cycle is broken.

Parents, it's time to teach our children to love their uniqueness. Let them know that their differences from their siblings make for an interesting conversation. Who wants to talk to people on a daily basis that are exactly like them? The conversation will become boring after awhile. Teach the child that if God wanted everyone and everything to look the same, He would not have created them as such. With all the different races in the world, God is not partial towards any.

Parents Show the Way

Parents, your deceptive ways will come back to haunt you, especially when it causes a rift between siblings. The Bible called Jacob a trickster (see Genesis 25-36). He learned this behavior from his mother, Rachael. She loved Jacob because he was a plain man and dwelled in tents, which means he avoided danger and tended to the sheep. Jacob's father, Isaac, favored Esau, the oldest son, because he loved the outdoors and ate what he killed. He was a man of the fields. Even today, men love their boys to be rough and tough, not soft and weak.

The tragedy to this story is that Jacob did not learn from his parents' mistakes. He carried this biased attitude into his family and ruined the relationship or bond that a father should have had with his boys. Jacob failed to break the cycle of partiality in his own home, which caused years of pain. One would think that after he saw the devastation that it caused between him and his brother, he would have tried to do things differently with his own children. But like Jacob, many of us will never learn until tragedy strikes.

Both parents were responsible for keeping the boys at odds with one another. They showed their love and loyalty to the child they favored the most. The boys saw this behavior in their parents and used it to their benefits—Jacob more so. When we as parents become partial when raising our kids, we may be teaching them how to be vindictive and manipulative, especially when they see it in us. Rachael taught her son, Jacob, these skills. Whenever Isaac spoke to Esau, Rachael would eavesdrop and inform Jacob of his father and brother's conversation. Rachael's philosophy was like many of ours today. Get ahead by any means necessary, even if we do not deserve it.

Like many of us, Jacob believed that he was entitled to things that did not belong to him. One day Esau had been in the field all day and was tired and hungry when he came home. Jacob had food to satisfy his brother's appetite but would not give him a bite to eat unless Esau sold him his birthright. Jacob learned how to be a con artist from his mother.

Siblings should support one another, not try to cheat and swindle each other. A selfish behavior between brothers and sisters will soon cause destruction within the family. Therefore, the kids learn how to take advantage of each other at any cost. As the children grow up, they believe that the only way to get ahead in life is to manipulate and trick their way into getting what they want. They never learned that there are consequences to a deceptive spirit. The people outside your family will not pamper you or tolerate your shady character.

Today we raise our kids to be competitive with one another. We praise the one that clawed his or her way to the top of the corporate ladder and show our disappointment with the one that is not quite as aggressive. At the family gatherings, it is always about what the successful one has accomplished, while belittling the one that has failed according to our standards of success. Is it right to tell our children that they are failures because their jobs do not meet our approval?

Rachael coerced Jacob to deceive his father by disguising himself as Esau. She wanted him to steal Esau's blessing. In the Bible days, when the father died, the eldest son would inherit all his wealth and rule over his house. Rachael would have no part of it, so she set her plans in motion for her favorite son to take charge. She refused to see her son bowing down to some rough-around-the-edges hunter. Rachael thought that Jacob was better than his brother was and did not want him to have to answer to Esau and be his slave. How could a mother stoop so low as to plot deceptions between her own two boys? Esau and Jacob were not strangers; they were her flesh and blood. As the story goes, these two brothers were in turmoil with each other from the time they exited their mother's womb.

After Jacob conned his father out of his brother's blessing, Esau hated Jacob to the point of plotting to kill him. When Rachael heard about Esau's anger, she told Jacob what he was planning to do. Rachael immediately packed his things and sent him away to her brother's house until Esau's anger cooled.

The Bible speaks a powerful truth, *"You will reap what you sow."* Jacob fell in love with a young girl name Rebekah. Her father would not allow the youngest girl to marry over the elder daughter, Leah. The Bible says, *"Leah was not an attractive woman and that Rebekah was beautiful. Therefore, Jacob loved her more."*

The trickster got tricked. When he thought that he was consummating his marriage with Rebekah, he unknowingly slept with Leah. The girls' father concealed Leah's identity by covering her face when Jacob entered the tent. What goes around comes back around in full circle. Leah's father disguised her just as Rachael had disguised Jacob. What you do unto others will eventually be done unto you. Now Jacob was stuck with Leah as his wife, and he had to work for their father another seven years before he could marry Rebekah.

In Jacob's marriages, there was favoritism shown between his two wives. When God saw how he hated Leah, He blessed her with numerous children while He closed Rebekah's womb. Jacob caused bitterness between these two sisters because he openly showed his love and affection towards Rebekah. Leah thought by conceiving many sons with Jacob it would make him love her, but it did not.

It is interesting how we can carry the deceptive ways of our childhood into our adult lives. Jacob grew up in a home of separation, and he carried this spirit into his marriages. It made one of his wives feel neglected and unwanted. Now we see how our behavior towards our children may cause them to grow up to be insensitive adults, thinking of no one but themselves, no matter whose feelings it hurts.

When parents raise children to be self-centered and believe that they are above others, it will cause those that cross their paths to get hurt. When Rachael finally conceived a son by Jacob, he failed to remember his past and what had separated him from his brother. Therefore, a wedge was torn between his firstborn by Rachael and Leah's children for years.

Children are a continuation of their parents. What legacy will we leave them? As parents, we are the first teachers that our kids see. Let us teach them to have values, to be honest, and to forgive. Children that possess these qualities will grow up to be adults that know how to repair relationships before they are damaged. Why? Because we, the parents, have taught them the basic rules for life—respect others, be trustworthy, and to treat others the way that they want to be treated.

Chapter Nine

Separating a Family

Joseph became the savior of his family because of his position in Pharaoh's palace. He was separated from his family for years because of the partiality that was showed towards him by his father. These problems could have been avoided if Jacob loved all his boys the same. Why would you buy one child an expensive coat and not the others? Did he ever stop to think about the results of his actions? Just think about how you would feel if someone treated you differently and thought that you were not worthy to be given the best. How would this affect you? What if the Savior of the world died only for others and not you? Would you harbor some bitterness inside? In your child's eyes, you are his or her savior first. So, when you show favoritism towards your kids, stop and think of the long-term effects. The results may be devastating.

Recognizing Children's Gifts

Look inside yourself as a parent to see if you are trying to make your child accomplish in life what you could not. Sometimes, parents will try to live their dreams through their children. This may cause them to fail or rebel because it's what you want and not the child. Not all kids are cut out to be doctors, scientists, lawyers, football players, movie stars, basketball players, or singers. Stop criticizing them for not wanting to live your dreams, and love and support each child equally for the path that they have chosen in life.

Our kids will find their niche in life if we, the parents, get out of the way. We are creating a world of dysfunctional children because we are trying to sway them in areas in their lives where they are not gifted. We refuse to allow them to explore the gifts that God has blessed them with because we believe them to be foolish. Someone has to be a soldier or a floor sweeper. Some of us tell our kids that it is demeaning when they work in these areas. If no one pursued these career choices, then our world would be an unprotected and filthy place.

Your child may have your genes and many of your features, but he or she is a unique individual, not a miniature you. Your job as a parent is to guide your children in the way that they should go, so when they are old, they will not depart from the lessons that you have taught them.

We are our children's first teacher. They learn from us, whether good or bad, and they mimic what they see us do. In their impressionable minds, we can do no wrong. When they see us being partial, they will think its okay to do so because Mommy or Daddy do it.

Kids are little people with feelings. No one can hurt or destroy a child the way a parent can. They look for us to love and protect them. Even when a child is being chastised, they should feel their parents' love.

God has left in His Word guidelines for us to follow when raising our children.

And now a word to you parents. Don't keep on scolding and nagging your children, making them angry and resentful. Rather, bring them up with the loving discipline the Lord himself approves, with suggestions and godly advice (Ephesians 6:4 TLB).

Parents, embrace your children's awkwardness and praise them when they try their best. In doing so, you will be showing them that it's okay to be themselves. Let them know that your love for them is forever and not conditional because as a parent you love their flaws and all. In doing these things you will know that the greatest job that God has given to men and women is parenthood.

Chapter Ten

Racism Within Races

Where is the newborn King of the Jews? for we have seen his star in far-off eastern lands, and have come to worship him (Matthew 2:2 TLB).

"Yes, in Bethlehem," they said, "for this is what the prophet Micah wrote: 'O little town of Bethlehem, you are not just an unimportant Judean village, for a Governor shall rise from you to rule my people Israel.'" Then, after being warned in a dream, he left for the region of Galilee. So the family went and lived in Nazareth. This fulfilled the prediction of the prophets concerning the Messiah, "He shall be called a Nazarene" (Matthew 2:5-6, 23 TLB).

Can you imagine being raised in a town where you are not expected to succeed? Just think for a moment, if you were the one that God chose to take a stand against those that judged others and abused their authority to oppress the poor. What if it was your own race that set traps to kill you because you had the courage to speak out and uncover their wickedness? Could you have handled the nasty stares, the gossip, the lies, and the violence—not from outsiders, but from your own? Well, guess what—Jesus stood against His own people when they thought that all He could be was a carpenter's son. They refused to believe that He was the Messiah that the prophet Isaiah had prophesied about hundreds of years earlier. Why? Because of whom his parents were and the town where they were born? It was even said by one of His future disciples, *"Can there any good thing come out of Nazareth?"* (John 1:46 KJV).

A child is innocent until poisonous words are spoken into his or her life. Who is that someone? What does that someone looks like? That someone is of his are her own race. Children learn about racism and prejudice first by those closest to them. They are the ones that have planted negative images in the child's life. Whether you are black, white, Hispanic, or Asian, that child sees someone that looks like him or her first.

Parents have taught their children how to discriminate within their race. Negative words are potent to growing children. They will grow up to be adults with all those stereotypical thoughts and images that have been planted within their minds by their parents. Seeds of hatred and prejudice against their race have been sown in their lives, which may cause them to struggle with issues of self-hatred when they get older. They were never taught that all of God's creation is beautiful and never encouraged to love and appreciate their own skin. All people are a part of Him no matter what nationality they may be. You should teach your children that they are wonderfully and perfectly made in Him because He is the perfect Lamb of God.

Racism within our own race has been passed down from generation to generation. It will never end until each race stops with what they think or believe to be wrong with them as a people. The way they speak, their education level, the neighborhoods they live in, and the complexion of their skin will always be the obstacles that keep them from moving forward if they do not learn to embrace and love the differences between themselves.

Each nationality has something negative or positive to say about each other, whether it's how they look, speak, or behave. Cliques are also formed within the races. If a person does not live up to the standards or expectations in that group, they will disassociate themselves from that person. In the black race, those that are light skinned have the tendency to hang out with those of like complexion and ostracize the darker group.

Paula was a single parent who was raising one biracial child and one black child. Family members and neighbors began to notice how she treated the biracial child differently from the other. The dark skinned child was poorly dressed and hair barely combed, while the biracial child had the best of everything.

One of Paula's friends asked her, "Why do you treat your light skinned child better than the darker one?" Paula replied, "Because she is prettier, her hair is long and wavy, and she's smarter." Her friend proceeded to ask, "What made you come to that conclusion?" Paula answered, "I was always taught that your skin color and hair defines your beauty and self-worth. You see it on television and in the magazines. Let's take it a step further; you see it also in our community."

Paula was a product of her environment. She believed that what she was doing was right. But little did Paula know that she was teaching her dark skin daughter that she was ugly and dumb because of the color of her skin.

Think about the long-term damage that this will cause if you allow a small factor, such as skin color and where a person comes from, to determine the self-worth of others as well as yourself. Have you ever stopped to think about what happened to the person that was affected by any prejudice or self-righteous attitude you may have shown? It's bad enough that prejudice and racism hurt when they come from outsiders, but they hurt worse when they come from someone of the same race. You expect to feel a sense of comfort and belonging when you are around those like you, but that is not the case with people that are dealing with this sensitive issue.

Your skin color or race is just a small part of who you really are. Your heart is what matters most to God and should also to man. Ask yourself, is your heart black and filled with hatred and prejudice? Or is it red, flowing with love and Jesus' blood? If so, then why are you discriminating against those that look different from you? Have you tried to get to know that person as an individual, instead of comparing him or her to others in his or her race that may have hurt you?

> *But the Lord said unto Samuel, Look not on his countenance, or on the height of his stature; because I have refused him: for the Lord seeth not as man seeth; for man looked on the outward appearance, but the Lord looketh on the heart* (1 Samuel 16:7 KJV).

One of the reasons that most people cannot get over the darkness or the lightness of a person's skin is because it makes them feel empowered to think that they are superior over another. It helps them to mask the hurt and pain that they have within themselves. Most people that show hate toward others in their race usually harbor self-hatred. They hate anything and anybody that remind them of themselves. The hurt and the taunting that were inflicted on them have now caused that person to do the same to others.

Will we ever get past the outer appearances of one another? When Jesus sees us, He sees the color red—His blood, His stamp of approval. That is the only color that matters to Him, not what side of the tracks we come from or our educational level. Why hurt one another over something as trivial as race, when in the end the only thing that Jesus will be looking for are those that are covered in His blood.

We tear each other apart; when we hurt, we want others to feel our pain. We allow meaningless things such as our skin color to block us from seeing the true beauty that Christ has placed within us all. Beauty starts on the inside and works itself on the outside, not the opposite. If we could change the darkness or lightness of our skin, would that make a difference in how we perceive others or ourselves? The answer is no, because we will always find a flaw. We must first love and see ourselves as God does in order to accept and love our differences. No matter what I change, if I cannot love myself, as Christ does, no amount of physical changes will help fill that void. Only the love of God can help me accept who I am and who He created me to be.

Racism does exist among blacks. We tear each other down when we fail to accept who we really are. God has created us in many different shades, and sadly, we often do not appreciate or embrace them. Many of us put each other down because of our short or kinky hair and dark complexion. Does that make us any less beautiful or appreciated if we possess these features?

We cling to every race except our own. If we have an ounce of mixed blood flowing through our veins, we will call out those races first before we would say black. African American is one of the most diverse races because of the many colors we possess, and yet we are ashamed to be who God created us to be.

Poor perception of oneself begins first at home within your family and race. We make negative racist comments towards each other, whether it's calling one another ignorant, black, or low-class because of our neighborhood. We as a people of color make differences among each other. Most grew up hating who they were for various reasons. When we show the world how we view each other as a people, they pick up on the negativity and throw it back in our faces. We become angry when others make racist and stereotypical comments about us, not realizing that we were the ones that gave them the ammunition. They are only mimicking what we think of one another.

If every race would love and value each other, how different the world would be. I can speak more candidly about the black race because I am a member of it. With other races, I can only talk about what I have witnessed in my own personal experiences. We may be different in skin color, but beneath, we are all the same—people that want to be comfortable in the skin that they were born in and not be made to feel ashamed because of it.

Most races believe that if your skin color is the same, it makes you closer. Nothing can be further from the truth. As a black race, most of us are separated from one another. We make differences, which are causing people to suffer in silence from the rejection of their peers. When a black has climbed the social ladder or come from an affluent family, they treat other blacks that have less as though they are plagued with a contagious disease. They even teach their kids that they are better and not to mingled with those from inner city neighborhoods. We are teaching our children that living in poverty makes them unimportant, and that only if they come from a nice neighborhood will their lives have value. A man or woman's character determines the type of person they are, not where they reside.

Some of the most influential blacks that had a part in shaping this great country came from impoverished neighborhoods. They broke the stigma that was placed on them by their own people. At times, we as a black race think that other races are the ones that are trying to keep us down, but in reality, we are the guilty ones. We hold each other down; when one rises above the poverty level, we take our foot and stomp—figuratively speaking—on the next person to keep them from doing the same. How can we expect others to treat us right when we have not learned how to do so ourselves?

God has a funny way of turning the tables; the same people that you stepped on while climbing up the ladder of success are the very same ones that you will see on your way back down that ladder. Those that considered themselves above others are now strung out on drugs and begging for handouts. It's not where you come from or the color of your skin that holds you back as a person, but ignorance. Success is built on faith in God, strong will, and determination. Living in the projects or a trailer park does not define you, but your will to survive and make a difference in society does. The color of your skin does not enslave you, but your attitude towards your environment and life is what oppresses you.

As a black race, we were taught that black folks do not get depressed or see psychiatrists. We were told to keep our business in our homes and in our neighborhoods. So, we swept our poor self-image and low self-esteem issues under the rug. We do not believe in exposing our personal business for the world to see, but our quietness has come back to haunt us. Our young girls are changing their appearance to look like women of other races because we have allowed others and our own race to tell them that short, nappy hair and dark black skin are not attractive. They bleach their hair and skin to obtain a look, so that those that have placed this burden of beauty on them will accept them. If God wanted them to have blue, hazel, or green eyes and bleached blonde hair, He would have made them with such. Whoever said blacks do not get depressed or suffer with a poor self-image spoke an untruth.

With the stigma that goes along with being black, a person must know who he or she is on the inside, or the opinions of others will cause that person to live a defeated and unproductive life. Understand that people put others down because they hate what they see in themselves. Their job is to make others feel as miserable and depressed as they feel.

We call each other degrading names that stick with many of us long after childhood. Why do we hurt one another? Are we not to edify and lift each other up the way that Christ said that we should? If so, then why do we become angry when others call us derogatory names when they have learned them from us?

For example, black men wanted to go on a rampage when a television commentary called a group of black female basketball players, "nappy headed hoes." My question to these black men is, where do you think this white man heard it from, and was that your first time hearing black women being called these degrading names? Black men, you often show your hatred and disgust of black women in your music and rap videos. You want a man of another race to be punished for the same vulgar language that you use each day to tear down black women.

How can a black woman love herself when she is made to feel inferior by the man that is supposed to be her king and put her on a pedestal? Why is she made to feel ashamed and worthless when her eyes are not blue and her hair is not blonde and straight? To cause a person in your own race to have such low self-esteem says a lot about you as a person. There is something that you hate about yourself when you try to make others feel ugly, unloved, and unwanted.

In the white communities, they make differences among each other as

57

Through the Eyes of God

well. If you are not a size zero thru four, blonde, tall, and slim, you are often not considered desirable or beautiful. If you live in a trailer park community, most upper-class whites will snub their noses at you and use the term, "white trash." They called people dumb hicks if they wear overalls and speak improper English.

I have seen white parents that have kids who are not old enough to know what overweight is, walking around with diet sodas and sandwich bags with only vegetables in them. I feel the message that is being sent to the child is that you will not be accepted by your peers if you do not look like them. Teaching good eating habits early is a good thing, but to tell a child that they won't be accepted because of what they look like is a different matter.

Yes, there is racism within the white race. It's not the person's fault that they cannot afford to live in a traditional home, but differences are made. Most upper-class whites are the same as upper-class blacks. If your family is not in the same income bracket or pursuing a higher education, they feel that you are beneath them. They also do not want their children to mix and mingle with kids that they feel are from the wrong side of the tracks—no matter how stable that person's family structure may be. I know and see these things happening because this is my reality living in the South. God never meant for any of us to turn our noses up or to think that we are better than others are. He said, *Let nothing be done through strife or vainglory; but in lowliness of mind let each esteem other better than themselves"* (Philippians 2:3 KJV).

Why do we thrive on hurting one another and pointing out one another's differences? Is it that difficult for us to see God in others? Is the color of our skin blinding us from seeing God's rainbow, which is arrayed in many colors? We are created in His image, and an image does not have a color but a reflection of what we desire to be. If we are created in His image, when we look at others, we should see His reflection in them. We as a race of people have so many debilitating hang-ups about each other that we cannot see the beauty that we each possess. We focus more on the outer appearances of others that we miss out on knowing the real person on the inside.

Racism within races is real. When we thrive on hurting and destroying one another because of it, there will be long-term damage. We must begin to make a conscious decision to change how we treat one another and realize that we need each other to survive. Satan is on the loose, and he is using the color of our skin as weapons of mass destruction. He knows that a racial war will get us off track from Jesus' instruction, *"Love thy neighbor as thyself"* (Galatians 5:14).

You are beautiful just the way you are. It's what's on the inside and not what's on the outside that makes you beautiful. Love your dark, fair, white, or brown complexion, because you are wonderfully and uniquely made. God took great pleasure in creating you; now it's time for you to believe it. The color of your skin is not what makes you beautiful, smart, or destined to succeed but it's your determination to break free from the stigma that has been attached to you by others.

Chapter Eleven

Prejudging Others

One day when Jesus was leaving the synagogue after teaching from the book of Isaiah, that He was indeed the Messiah, His own people spat on Him and ripped His clothing. They would have thrown Jesus over a cliff if He had not escaped by pushing His way through the angry crowd. But, Jesus did not let it sidetrack Him from His mission.

We often allow negative comments to detour us from following the course that God has laid out for our lives. We become depressed or worried about the prejudice attitude of others towards us. What if Jesus would have listened to people when they called Him a lover of the Gentiles—people of a mixed race? What if He would have let the name calling and threats keep Him from going to Calvary? If Jesus decided to die for His race, what hope would non-Jews have?

"How is this possible?" the people exclaimed. "He's just a carpenter's son, and we know Mary his mother and his brothers—James, Joseph, Simon, and Judas. And his sisters—they all live here. How can he be so great?" And they became angry with him! (Matthew 13:55-57 TLB).

People that knew Jesus as a child found it hard to believe that He had so much wisdom concerning the Scriptures and could perform miracles. These men could not see past the familiarity. Therefore, they became closed minded to Jesus being the promised Savior. They refused to believe that He came through the lineage of King David. And they could not imagine that it was He that Isaiah and other prophets had prophesied about hundreds of years earlier. In their minds, Jesus showed no resembles to the conquering king that they expected. Surely, their king would not be a scrawny, uneducated carpenter's son. Perception can be misleading. God uses what man believes to be nothing and turns it into something great.

Then Jesus told them, "A prophet is honored everywhere except in his own country, and among his own people!" (Matthew 13:57 TLB).

Do not let what you think you know about someone cause you to close your heart and mind to the fact that God is working through them. Oftentimes, it's your own family that will doubt what God is doing through you. God will bless you with children that are gifted in many areas; but you, their own parents, will discourage them from exploring and enhancing those gifts. You would tell them that they are too ugly to be in front of the camera, and they need to find a career that is safe, where people will not judge them on their looks or color. Or you might say that they are too fat to do this or that; they need to lose a few pounds. You also look at where a person comes from, whether it's from the inner cities, the projects, or the trailer park, and try to discourage them from following their dreams of becoming the first college graduate from their neighborhood or family. Who knows what a person can accomplish with a little encouragement and faith? It has to start with those from their own home first. Starting with your own home or country is taught throughout the Bible, because before you can teach someone else about loving themselves and others, you must first love and treat your own with the love and the respect they deserve.

Hold your head up high and know that Satan is the driving force behind hatred and bigotry. Many will never break the cycle of prejudging others, but you do not have to let it destroy and rule your life. When people see you trying to break free from the stereotypes that have been placed on you, they will do and say everything to keep you believing those lies. Jesus is your best example. He could have given in to the stereotypes and allowed it to keep Him from saving humanity, but He kept His eyes on the prize—bringing all men together as one.

I have experienced this in my own life; at times, it will be your own that will try to hold you back. Many people will tell you untruths about yourself to distract you from moving forward. They see the potential in you, but they do not want you to achieve it. Therefore, they will try to break your self-esteem level down to make you feel inferior. They will use your insecurities as ammunition against you.

Jesus was not reverenced in His own country or home. He outraged His people for speaking the truth about His deity. The people focused more on where Jesus came from— Nazareth—and who His parents were, than the Word that He spoke. Jealousy was one of the problems because Jesus had the ability to capture the crowd's attention by the way He spoke God's Words. The leaders knew that they could not compete with Jesus' wisdom when it came to the Word of God. So, they resorted to calling Jesus a Beelzebub—or a crazy person.

> *But the Jewish teachers of religion who had arrived from Jerusalem said, "His trouble is that he's possessed by Satan, king of demons. That's why demons obey him." Jesus summoned these men and asked them (using proverbs they all understood), "How can Satan cast out Satan? A kingdom divided against itself will collapse. A home filled with strife and division destroys itself. And if Satan is fighting against himself, how can he accomplish anything? He would never survive. [Satan must be bound before his demons are cast out], just as a strong man must be tied up before his house can be ransacked and his property robbed* (Mark 3:22-27 TLB).

A nation divided cannot stand. So, don't be caught off guard when your relatives try to put an end to the plans that God has for your life. If Jesus' family and countrymen could not stop Him from fulfilling the plans that God had for His life, then neither can yours. Know that you are a child of God and stay on the path that He has chosen for you. What if singers, movie stars, and ministers would have believed what people had told them? The world would have never had the blessing of being touched by their lives and their stories. They made it over the obstacles of poverty because they saw themselves as God saw them: talented, gifted, anointed, intelligent, and destined to succeed.

They refused to believe the negative garbage that was fed to them by others. Many families and communities believe and teach that if you were born poor, then you will always be that way—but whose report are you going to believe?

Proving others wrong should motivate you to want to break the cycle of ignorance and racism. Believe in God first and believe in yourself last, and then you will see Him opening doors that were once closed to you. No matter what racial background you come from, Jesus has blessed you to rise above every obstacle that has been placed in your life. "*Thou hast caused men to ride over our heads; we went through fire and through water: but thou broughtest us out into a wealthy place*" (Psalms 66:12 KJV).

The color of your skin has no value with God, but what is valuable to Him is that you love your neighbor—black, white, yellow, or brown—as yourself. When you spend time hating and separating yourself from others because of their differences, the Lord is grieved. It is He that created you to be the person that you are. When you make derogatory comments about another race or your own, you are simply telling God that He made a mistake in what He has created.

I believe that when God made the different shades of colors, He knew that He had a mixture that was so beautiful that nothing could ever compare to it. All of them blended so well together, but we are the ones that have taken those exquisite colors that God has made and turned them into something ugly. We turned them into something ghastly and undesirable when we began attaching negative names to them. I believe that God is sitting in heaven and looking down on us and wondering how could something that started out so lovely turn into chaos. It all began when one color wanted to be superior over the others. Remember Lucifer and how he wanted to be mightier than God was.

Man is responsible for the color wars. We have caused others to be ashamed about how God has created them. Families are isolating other family members if they look a certain way. Communities are saying, "We have to be just the right shade of brown or white to be beautiful." We will never live in harmony until we see each other as the same. Prejudging others was never God's intentions when He made us different from each other.

I realized one thing while writing this book: we all stand accused of prejudging others at some point and time in our lives—intentionally or unintentionally. This behavior will cause serious problems for future generations if we do not learn from our mistakes. Whether we want to believe it or not, our children are paying attention to how we reject others when they do not fit into our superficial beauty or intellectual category.

We need to teach our young children that to make it in this world, they must strive to do their best, believe in themselves, and always trust God to order their steps in life. Stop lying to them that their looks or skin color will get them where they need to be. Beauty will fade. King Solomon spoke it when he said, "*Favor is deceitful, and beauty is vain*" (Proverbs 31:30 KJV). If we do not educate our impressionable kids while they are young, we as parents will leave the door open for others to come in and poison their minds with racial garbage against others.

Have we become so consumed with perfection and perception that we have lost our ability to love and accept one another's flaws? People have a hard time dealing with life itself, but when we throw race into the equation, more pressures are added.

Did it hurt when Jesus' hometown rejected Him? Yes, it hurt Him to know that His own rejected and despised Him, but what could He do about the situation? He stayed focused, showed love, and followed the Father's will all the way to Calvary. So stop allowing your own race, as well as other races, to label and define you. Stop looking in the mirror feeling ashamed of who you are. God has great things in store for you. Your community, family, or race has nothing to do with your success in life. The only person that can stop you is you. Rise above the negative stereotypes that others have labeled you to be. Look into your spiritual mirror. In this mirror, God will show you how beautiful and wonderful your soul—not skin color—is to Him. In this mirror, you will be looking at the face of God because when you look at yourself, you will see His image staring back at you. In Him there are no mistakes, only a perfect vessel waiting to be used.

Families and communities may leave you broken, but only a true and living God has the ability to take your broken soul and mend it together again. So what if your skin is dark as the night or white as the snow. God foreknew what color He wanted you to be. Your own may criticize you, but God embraces your individuality, He knows what lies beneath the color of your skin. He knows that there is more to you than what meets the eye.

Be proud of who you are, because there will never be another you. Those who prejudge you because of the color of your skin have been hurt at some point in their lives and are becoming like the person who criticized them. They themselves have grown up to be insecure about their own complexion. Now they are taking their frustrations out on their children and those around them with negative comments. They fail to see that life is like a pattern or circle. If the race-on-race hatred is not broken, the same hurt that they inflicted on others will continue.

Prejudging Others

When God created us different—in color only—He never meant for us to take those differences to prejudge others. When we criticize others because of his or her skin color or race, we are saying that we have insecurities. Black-on-black racism, white-on-white racism, and so forth, will never end until we all believe that we come from the same race—the human race—under one God and one nation with liberty and justice for all.

Learn to be a compassionate lover of all men. Do not close your heart and mind to those that are different from you because you will miss out on the best that God has to offer. The time is now to get to know those whom you have been avoiding because of skin color. Who knows? You just might find out that you have more in common than you thought.

Chapter Twelve

The Color of Beauty

. . . whence came all these people? They are a mixture of English, Scotch, Irish, French, Dutch, German, Swedes . . . What, then is the American, this new man? He is neither an European nor the descendent of an European; hence that strange mixture of blood, which you will find in no other country. I could point out to you a family whose grandfather was an Englishman, whose wife was Dutch, whose son married a French woman, and whose present four sons have now four wives of different nations. He is an American, who leaving behind him all his ancient prejudices, and manners, receives new ones from the new mode of life he has embraced, the new government he obeys, and the new rank he holds . . . The Americans were once scattered all over Europe; here they are incorporated into one of the finest systems of populations which has ever appeared (Hector St. Jean de Crevecoeur, 18th century commentator on America).

The color of beauty is a mixture of races and nationalities blended into one large melting pot, to form one of the most beauty colors ever known to man—red—the color of Jesus' blood. But, someone believed that one color was more beautiful than all the rest and distorted this beauty. God colored our outsides differently so when we look at each other, we will see the unique beauty that we each display. But He made the blood that flows through our veins to be the same—red. The blood connects us together because it was His Son's sacrificial gift to men. It was shed to atone for our sins that once disconnected and estranged us from God.

We have allowed Satan to tarnish and blind our view of how we see each color as being beautiful. He wants us to believe that something is wrong with us if we are too light, too dark, or too in between. He floods our minds with many types of images, such as self-doubt and insecurities about the colors that God has created us to be.

We as humans spend too much time and energy on the exterior of a person that we forget that there is much more to him or her internally just waiting to be explored. When we cannot get past the color of a person's skin, it hinders us from seeing the beauty that God has placed in him or her.

When the world becomes color blind, then and only then will we be able to live harmoniously with one another. Judging others by the color of their skin gets in the way of discovering who they really are—rare diamonds, priceless jewels.

I can only imagine how all the immigrants felt that traveled to Anderson Island and saw that great lady—the Statue of Liberty, holding her touch, which represents liberty and justice for all. She embodies the idea that everyone will be treated equally and have the same opportunities. Unfortunately, many times these people were told that they were not the right color or nationality. As the great melting pot, with all races mixed together to create one color, one nation, many immigrants experienced rejection from Americans who believed these foreigners would taint and distort the whole pot.

J. Hector St. John De Crevecoeur could not have said it better, this new man was, *"leaving behind him all his ancient prejudices and manners. Here individuals of all races are melted into a new race of man, whose labors and posterity will one day cause great changes in the world."*

To be melted as one man is to be of the same mind, the same body, and the same soul—to be in one accord. We should look for strength in each other to come together as one race under God's rules. I do not believe that Crevecoeur meant that when the colors were melted or blended together that it was right to leave out the ones that we thought were ugly and useless. I know that it was not what God meant when He created us to live with one another in one land, one country, and under one heaven.

*Favor is deceitful, and beauty is vai*n (Proverbs 31:30 KJV).

We have all heard the expression that beauty is skin deep; it's skin deep because our physical beauty will eventually fade, but God sees the beauty that lies deep within us. Favor is deceitful because it will fool us into believing that people love us because of who we are, when in reality it was what they saw on the outside that kept us in their good graces. Time always brings about a change, and when time takes away our beauty, the favor that we once received will come to an end because it was contingent on what was on the outside and not the beauty that lies beneath our physical exterior.

To God, the color of your skin does not matter when your insides are corroded with hatred and malice toward those that are different. If you could see yourself through the eyes of God, what reflection or color would you see staring back at you? Would it be green, the color of envy, or would it be black, a heart that is dark as the night?

Jesus talked with the woman at Jacob's well about the Living Water—the Holy Spirit (see John 4)—but when His disciples saw Him, they could not believe that He was talking to her because she was different. They did not know that the gospel would be for all men and women, not just for those like themselves. Jesus had to teach His disciples to let go of past hang-ups because there were a lot of people who were different from them. To me, Jesus was saying, "This is a new day, a day that all men would be looked upon as one."

When God looks at your soul, He will not be checking for the color of your skin at the gate but how well you treated all men as yourself. King Solomon penned it best when he said, *"Favor is deceitful."* It is deceitful because Satan has put blinders on you so that you cannot see the sign ahead that says, "No colors allowed in heaven, only bloodstained souls dripping with My Son's blood."

Can your beauty teach you how to love or to have a compassionate heart? When you allow Satan to put you on a pedestal of lies, you will be deceived into believing that others are beneath you. He showers you with gifts, causing you to be full of yourself, only to kick the pedestal from underneath you when the next great thing comes along. Ask yourself this question, "Can my beauty or skin color save my soul?"

People use the color of their skin to think more highly of themselves than they should. Don't they know that when Jesus returns, He will seek those that bear one of His most important characteristics—love? Next, He will seek out those that bear the emblem red, revealing those that have lived and died in Christ. Skin color will not matter. We fight and argue on this side of life that "black is beautiful" and "white means power." What beauty or power will we have when Jesus comes to claim our souls, if we are not covered in His blood? There are no segregated sections in heaven.

Real Beauty

A person's heart and the kindness of his or her soul should determine that individual's beauty. Some people may look spectacular in person, but when they open their mouths, we cannot wait to get away from them. We do so because of the ugliness of their heart and their mistreatment of others. Jesus said, *"Do not ye yet understand, that whatsoever entereth in at the mouth goeth into the belly, and is cast out into the draught? But those things which proceed out of the mouth come forth from the heart; and they defile the man"* (Matthew 15:17-18 KJV). Jesus wanted His disciples to know that the heart is where evil lives. *"For out of the heart proceed evil thoughts"* (Matthew 15:19 KJV). A man's skin color does not make him evil because it does not have the ability to destroy another's self-esteem or self-worth. We destroy one another with loathing words that come from our mouths. It makes us ugly through and through when those words are spoken from a hateful heart.

Beauty is in the eyes of the beholder, and the beholder is God, who made all things. If He made all things beautiful, how does one's color determine beauty? Did God make a mistake when He painted us with the strokes of His fingertips? Did He spill a color over onto the others and taint them? Was it meant to be something else? The color of beauty is like the rainbow—although there may be many colors, they're all beautiful when added together. God does not love or think one color is more worthy than the others are, and He does not create anything by mistake. All things are wonderfully and perfectly made because He made them all.

Who distorted God's perfect rainbow? When man looked at the colors, he began to pass judgment on the ones that he did not consider attractive. Man began spreading hateful rumors and lies that God had made a mistake by placing one of the colors next to the others. Man made the other colors start passing judgment on the one that did not fit into his array of beauty. Therefore, one of the colors was rejected and criticized for not looking or measuring up to the others and was removed from the remaining colors of the rainbow, which in turn ruined God's perfect picture of true beauty.

Jesus touched many lives in His three-and-a-half years of teaching here on earth. He taught us how to look past a man's race or nationality and see that there is much more to him or her than skin color and racial background. Jesus knew that the changing of a man's heart was more important than his skin color. People from His own race could not understand why He dealt with or was concerned for others that were different from Him. In due time they would be shocked to learn that He came to earth to save all that would believe and look upon Him for salvation. He did not come to overthrow the Roman government, which had the Jews in bondage at that time, but to give men spiritual liberty.

Jesus broke the color barrier when He took the time to share His saving grace to those of other nationalities. He set the example of how to look past a man's outer appearance to find the true beauty of his soul. Jesus touched the lives of people of different nations and countries such as the Greeks, Gentiles, Samaritans, and the Syro Phoencians. Each of these groups thought it strange that a Jew would sit down to a conversation with them about spiritual things. It was common knowledge that the Jews had no dealings with them because of their nationality.

> *Soon a Samaritan woman came to draw water, and Jesus asked her for a drink. He was alone at the time as his disciples had gone into the village to buy some food. The woman was surprised that a Jew would ask a "despised Samaritan" for anything— usually they wouldn't even speak to them!—and she remarked about this to Jesus. He replied, "If you only knew what a wonderful gift God has for you"* (John 4:7-10 TLB).

We need to recognize all the wonderful characteristics about each other, but we have allowed something as minute as color to stand in the way. The Samaritans were belittled and looked down upon because they were considered unclean. The Jews did not drink or eat from a Samaritan dish because they thought that it would make them ceremonially unclean.

Jesus had good news for this Samaritan woman. He was preparing her for a life-changing experience. The isolation and segregation of religion and race that she once experienced in her life would become a thing of the past. The gospel that was preached first to the Jews would be for people of all colors and races.

Jesus wanted her to know that she was just as much entitled to the truth of His saving grace as the next person. All He required of her was belief and faith in Him. The Samaritan woman was so grateful that she ran and told everyone she met. Truly, this was a new day, where all colors and classes of people would have to acknowledge Jesus in order be accepted into His kingdom.

Color of Beauty

Have you ever noticed the myriad of colors in a quilt? With all the mismatched colors, it should be one of the ugliest things that you have ever seen—but not so. The different colors and patterns are what make the quilt beautiful and unique.

Now look at the different colors that God has knitted together. Are we not more beautiful than that of a quilt? Why do we feel that our color is ugly or all wrong when we do not look like the rest? Is the myriad of colors in a quilt more beautiful and admired more than that of the multitudes of colors in living and breathing humans? Some of us can mix and match the many colors of a quilt together and call it beautiful but cannot look at each other and say the same.

The color of beauty is you and I mixed together with the love of God. He mixed and matched us together like that of a pattern in a quilt. If one color to that pattern is missing or left out on purpose, it ceases to be beautiful.

Instead, we will lovingly follow the truth at all times—speaking truly, dealing truly, living truly—and so become more and more in every way like Christ who is the Head of his body, the church. Under his direction the whole body is fitted together perfectly, and each part in its own special way helps the others parts, so that the whole body is healthy and growing and full of love (Ephesians 4:15-16 TLB).

Will the color war ever end? One can only hope. Being diverse was never meant to separate or make anyone superior over the other, but we are to work and live together as one man, spreading the gospel of Jesus Christ. The preaching of Jesus has been hindered because we focus more on our differences and spread hate against each other.

Out of all God's creation, man is the only one that shows partiality due to color. When birds fly together, they do not say to the others, "You cannot fly with us, because you are different." Dogs, when they play and chase one another, do not say to the other dogs, "You cannot play or chase after us because you look different." All that these animals see is another bird or dog. So, why is it hard for people to see one another as humans rather than a color?

Should I be judged by my color because it's not like yours? When you treat me differently, it hurts. When you say derogatory things about my color, it stings. When you think or believe that I am a certain way because of the color of my skin, it makes me feel ashamed of the person that God has created me to be. Your words make me feel ugly and unattractive when I am compared to those that are different from me. Is my color not beautiful because it's not like yours?

The color of beauty is truly a mixture of all races and nationalities combined together. We are all unique and beautiful in our own way, because it's our diversities that make us so. God knitted and fitted us together perfectly, and each part in its own special way helps the other parts so that our minds, bodies, and souls are healthy and growing with love for one another. Love the skin that you are in because beauty comes in all shades and colors.

Chapter Thirteen

Overcoming Your Prejudice

Peter told them, "You know it is against the Jewish laws for me to come into a Gentile home like this. But God has shown me in a vision that I should never think of anyone as inferior" (Acts 10:28 TLB).

Amazingly, God can change the way that a man thinks just by revealing his bigotry and prejudices through a dream. Peter was asleep on a rooftop when God showed him how prejudiced he was, and He used animals that were considered unclean and uncommon according to the Mosaic Law as an example. God wanted to teach Peter a valuable lesson about prejudging others before knowing them.

In his dream, God was preparing Peter for a meeting with Cornelius who was not a Jew. God knew that Peter would be one of the apostles to carry the gospel to non-Jews. Peter was responsible for teaching Cornelius and his entire house about the saving grace of Jesus Christ.

God was teaching Peter to let go of what he was taught from childhood concerning those that were different from him. He wanted Peter to know and understand that salvation is for all men. God would not be just if He saved one race and caused the others to perish without a chance to accept His Son as their Savior.

Now all of us, whether Jews or Gentiles, may come to God the Father with the Holy Spirit's help because of what Christ has done for us. Now you are no longer strangers to God and foreigners to heaven, but you are members of God's very own family, citizens of God's country, and you belong in God's household with every other Christian. What a founda-

tion you stand on now: the apostles and the prophets; and the cornerstone of the building is Jesus Christ himself! We who believe are carefully joined together with Christ as parts of a beautiful, constantly growing temple for God. And you also are joined with him and with each other by the Spirit, and are part of this dwelling place of God (Ephesians 2:18-22 TLB).

Thank God that Peter was obedient; he would have missed a valuable opportunity to witness Jesus to the unsaved if he had not overcome his prejudiced ways. Discrimination only keeps us from seeing that we all need Jesus to save our souls from an impending damnation. We all feel the pain of segregation and many will never recover from the devastation of it. Peter had to overcome his prejudices concerning those of another race and learn that every man deserves the opportunity to hear and learn about Jesus Christ.

How can we reach those that are different from us if we cannot get past the color of their skin? Are they not deserving of the gospel that has the ability to change the way a man thinks and sees others? Of what are we afraid? Does he or she not have two eyes, two arms, or two legs? Does being a certain color qualify a person for being more human than the next?

When we cannot see past a person's race or color, it becomes a stumbling block to our spiritual growth. And when we cease to grow, our minds will not allow us to see the beauty that we each possess. Our color keeps us from fellowshipping with each other; it makes us pass by one another without speaking or acknowledging each other's presence. Many of us are afraid to sit by other races for fear that their color will rub off and contaminate us. Eventually, racism and prejudice will destroy us if we do not overcome them.

We oppress one another because of skin color. That is where the name-calling began, along with separating ourselves. The only thing that the Father wanted us to separate ourselves from was sin, not each other.

Peter slipped momentarily into his old way of thinking. He continued to take the Word of God to the Gentiles. The problem came when he was eating with some non-Jewish brothers in Antioch and became hypocritical in their presence. How can one win souls when one's attitude changes when those of another race enter onto the scene?

But when Peter came to Antioch I had to oppose him publicly, speaking strongly against what he was doing for it was very wrong. For when he first arrived he ate with the Gentile Christians [who don't bother with circumcision and the many other Jewish laws]. But afterwards when some Jewish friends came, he wouldn't eat with the Gentiles anymore because he was afraid of what these Jewish legalists, who insisted that circumcision was necessary for Salvation, would say; and then all the other Jewish Christian and even Barnabas became a hypocrites too, followed Peter's example, though they certainly knew better (Galatians 2:11-13 TLB).

Our behavior at times are like that of Peter. People are dying all over the world, lost in their sins, because we fail to help them due to the color of their skin. What a sad world we live in, when we cannot look past race to save a brother or a sister that is on the way to hell. In hell, there will be all races and nationalities. Do not be deceived into thinking that only the color that looks like you will be in heaven and all others will be in hell. There are people that believe this untruth. Heaven and hell will be full of all races and classes of people. There is room for all in both places, but why would someone want to end up losing his or her soul because of something that is as ridiculous as racism.

Peter had to be reprimanded by the apostle Paul for his actions, because it could have easily led someone away from Christ. How can you win someone over, when you alienate yourself from him or her when friends come to town? How do you expect them to feel? Are they not worthy to be seen in public with you or introduced to your friends? If they are good enough to teach Jesus to, then they should be good enough to socialize with in public.

We need to make a conscious effort not to become hypocritical when we preach Jesus to those that are of another race. Whether we know it are not, people are watching and waiting to see if we are living what we preach. How can we preach, "Love your neighbor as yourself," but hate the very people that we want to accept our Savior? As teachers and laborers of the Word, we need to set a better example because God's gospel is not a segregated gospel.

We need to do more to reach out and witness to others, instead of staying in our comfort zones. The time is now to break the color barriers and deliver God's message to all races, so that they will turn from a life of sin. How can we that know the truth sit back and watch someone that is of another race die without giving them an opportunity to accept Jesus as his or her Savior? How dare we pick and choose the ones that we think deserves salvation over the other!

Peter learned a very valuable lesson not to judge a man by the color of his skin and his neighborhood. Those that are seeking the truth about Jesus are looking for genuine people that know the truth to teach and preach it to them. Peter had to learn that Jesus taught him and the other disciples so that they may in turn carry the gospel to all creeds, nations, and races.

We should be careful when we segregate ourselves from others because it maybe those that we least expect to come to our aid and rescue us in our times of need. The Good Samaritan did just that. The Samaritans were looked down on because they were people of a mixed race. But what happened to a certain man on the road from Jerusalem to Jericho that day proved that those that think themselves to be good stewards turned out to be the least of them when it came to giving an injured man a helping hand.

And Jesus answering said, A certain man went down from Jerusalem to Jericho, fell among thieves, which stripped him among of his raiment, and wounded him, and departed, leaving him half dead. And by chance there came down a certain priest that way: and when he saw him, he passed by on the other side. And likewise a Levite, when he was at the place, came and looked on him, and passed by on the other side. But a certain Samaritan, as he journeyed, came where he was: and when he say him, he had compassion on him (Luke 10:30-33 KJV).

Jesus asked a certain lawyer, "Which now of these three, thinkest thou, was neighbour unto him that fell among the thieves?" Jesus went on to tell him and the crowd that was standing by that the men that failed to lend a helping hand to the wounded man were priests and Levites—men that were learned in the Mosaic Law and who should have known better. These men were responsible for offering sacrifices to the Lord for the nation of Israel's sins, yet they refused to give aid to a man barely clinging to life.

How could this be? These were the caretakers of the Israelites' souls, and yet they saw a man lying on a dusty road like a dead dog and kept on walking by as if he were nothing. However, Jesus used this parable to illustrate to us how we put ourselves above others because of who we think we are. When it came down it, it was the one we thought the least of that showed the love of Christ. The Samaritans were treated like the filth of the earth, but this Samaritan was the only one that showed compassion to this injured stranger.

When Jesus finished teaching about the Good Samaritan, He told the man to go and do likewise. He wanted everyone to show mercy and compassion towards all men, not to just those that they felt were the same as they were.

We have seen in this parable with the Good Samaritan that he was considered the least expected to lend a helping hand. He didn't just take the wounded man to safety; he paid for his room and board and offered to pay extra if it was not enough. But the ones that knew God's Word were the very ones that left him for dead on the side of the road. A person's race does not make him righteous, but it's his compassionate heart to help strangers when they have fallen prey to tragedy or hard times.

Jesus was not just talking to the certain lawyer to do likewise. We have a responsibility today to do the same. When I come to your aid, I should look past your skin color and assist your needs because you are my sister or brother in Christ. I am to follow the example that He has left for us.

What type of person will you or I be, if a man lies dying in the streets and we refuse to get him help because of his race? Could you live with yourself or look in the mirror knowing that you let a man die because his color was not the same as yours?

When Jesus spoke to His disciples and other followers, He wanted to make sure that they overcame their prejudice of others. Jesus taught His disciples three-and-a-half years so that they could take His gospel to all people—not a few select groups. He went to Calvary so everyone can have the same opportunity to accept Him as their Savior. We can truly say that Jesus saw the beauty in all men when He decided to give up His life. When He was nailed to the cross, He saw people not the color of their skin; he saw souls that needed His blood for the atonement of their sins.

Kirk Franklin released a song a couple of years ago, which expressed that the color of your skin does not matter as long as your blood is red. The blood of Jesus will teach me how to love those that are different. Because His blood flows like a river through my veins, it teaches me not to judge what is seen on the surface but to look deeper. The blood helps me to get past my ignorance of others. The blood of Jesus broke all color barriers two thousand years ago so that all men can have the same chance of a better life. When we see the Spirit of God in others, we have witnessed what true beauty is. We see no black man, no white man, and no brown man when we overcome our prejudice. We only see the color red from Jesus' crucified blood that is now branded on those that have accepted Him as their Lord and Savior.

Jesus' blood is strong enough to take away any form of hatred that you may have against others that are different from you. It's pure enough to change a heart that is filled with self-righteousness. The blood of Jesus has the power to change a man's thought process that was once taught separatism. God has the power, not you, to change the way you see your brother or sister that sit next to you every day. First John 4:20 (TLB) says, *"If anyone says 'I love God,' but keeps on hating his brother, he is a liar; for if he doesn't love his brother who is right there in front of him, how can he love God whom he has never seen?"* It should be easier to love someone that you have seen versus someone you have not. But you do it day after day when you see someone of another race and say that you hate him or her because of it.

Pentecost Unified the Multitudes

On the day of Pentecost, there were one hundred and twenty people from all racial backgrounds. They were there to enjoy the celebration, but they found themselves seeing and experiencing a miracle that would change the face of mankind forever. The truth that had been concealed from those of the non-Jewish faith was about to enlighten them to the awesome power of God.

When the Spirit of the Lord showed up on that day, all the people there heard what was happening in their own language. All men heard the blessings of the Lord in their native tongue. They knew and understood that something supernatural was taking place. No longer would the secrets of God be concealed from them. They knew that the message preached that day would be for all races and generations to come.

God never meant for the gospel to be hidden from the Gentiles forever. He had to prepare the hearts and minds of His people first, the Jews. The Scripture says, *"The multitude of them that believed were of one heart and of one soul: neither said any of them that ought of the things which he possessed was his own; but they had all things in common"* (Acts 4:32 KJV). The Day of

Pentecost brought all nationalities together to celebrate the beginning of fellowshipping as one. No one segregated themselves from the others.

The multitude was unified on that special day. What happened throughout the years that separated us from staying as one mind and one soul? False teachers were filled with hate and determined to destroy what God had ordained—unity among one another as one people, with one mind, and one cause. They have turned it into a color war. They believed that we should stick with our own kind and share God's words with those that look like us.

We have allowed these false teachers to come in and spread prejudice and hate among us. They have come up with demeaning names to make others feel insecure and rejected as a people. These teachers of hate have destroyed the beauty and the uniqueness of God's creation. They preached that separatism is right and mingling with outsiders will contaminate the color that they believed to be superior over them all. The false teachers preached lies, deceit, and hatred. How can one color be classified as the color of beauty, when they all came from God?

Then shall the dust return to the earth as it was: and the spirit shall return unto God who gave it. Vanity of vanities, saith the preacher; all is vanity (Ecclesiastes 12:7-8 KJV).

King Solomon said it best when he declared that all the things that we argue or fight over on earth are futile because they will all pass away. Fighting over which color is the prettiest will soon cease. When all is said and done, we will all turn back into the dust from whence we came. Then, what will become of the color of beauty—if there is such a one? All that matters in the end is where your soul will return. Will it remit to its Creator or will it go to the one that made your color the most important thing in your life—Satan, the master of deception.

King Solomon said that there is nothing new under the sun. The things we argue over now were argued over in his day. We are not the first generation to prejudge others. It will always exist until our spirits return to God and our flesh to the dirt. Vanity of vanities, said the preacher, it's all vanity.

What then is the American, this new man? He is an American, who, leaving behind him all his ancient prejudices and manners, receives new ones from the new mode of life he has embraced, the new government he obeys, and the new rank he holds. He has become an American by being received in the broad lap of our great alma mater. Here individuals of all races are melted into a new race of man, whose labors and posterity will one day cause changes in the world (J. Hector St. John De Crevecoeur).

Chapter Fourteen

Overweight

Wherefore seeing we also are compassed about with so great a cloud of witnesses, let us lay aside every weight, and the sin which doth so easily beset us, and let us run with patience the race that is set before us, looking unto Jesus the author and finisher of our faith; who for the joy that was set before him endured the cross, despising the shame, and is set down at the right hand of the throne of God (Hebrews 12:1-2 KJV).

A "cloud of witnesses" are those saints that have died and are therefore witnessing the struggles that we are facing while running this competitive race called life. The writer is saying that they had run the same race and won. He is encouraging us to hold on; we shouldn't quit because the finish line is just a few steps ahead.

We know that bad eating habits have a way of packing on the pounds, but so does allowing others to feed us bad information; it adds weight, mentally and spiritually. Some of that bad information includes the studies that are taken by others that tell us which categories we fall within when it comes to fitting into America the beautiful. If we overindulge on what is said about us, weights such as depression, loneliness, poor self-image, and low self-esteem can develop.

Just how does the Hebrew writer propose that we lay aside these weights when it feels as if the world hates us because of how we look? The difficulty comes when we are tipping the scale with feelings of despair. We stress over images that show us what body sizes are acceptable and what are not. Therefore, we overindulge in buying what we think will be the remedy for our weight problems.

We allow the bumps and bruises in life to burden us. Bitterness, bad re-lationships, incest, rape, verbal abuse, and physical abuse are bumps and bruises that keep us out of the race. We must learn how to turn our prob-lems over to God. He is our healer. Many times, we talk to psychiatrists only to feel worse about ourselves afterwards. Only God has the ability to heal us from the weight of this world. He wants to carry all our burdens so that we can run this race free from the sins that are set to entangle us. He understands that the weights will cause us to stumble and fall because they have accumulated over the years from overeating on the junk that society has fed us about ourselves.

We complain about the extra pounds that we have gained over the years from taking in negative conversation, but we fail to do anything to lose them. First, we must stop eating garbage from those that try to keep us thinking negatively about ourselves. To lay aside every weight, you must be willing to lose hindering spirits that will keep you from seeing yourself as God does.

When people try to pull you down instead of helping you up, they be-come a hindrance. They were placed in your life by Satan to make you give up on the race for your peace of mind, your sanity, and your self-worth. He makes you question these things in your life. Satan's job is to destroy you. He adds the weight on so that you will buckle under pressure. Satan thrives on your depression, low self-esteem, and negative spirit, which symbolizes human defeat.

> *Keep your eyes on Jesus, our leader and instructor. He was willing to die a shameful death on the cross because of the joy he knew would be his af-terwards; and now he sits in the place of honor by the throne of God. If you want to keep from becoming fainthearted and weary, think about his patience as sinful men did such terrible things to him. After all, you have never yet struggled against sin and temptation until you sweat great drops of blood* (Hebrews 12:2-4 TLB).

Jesus set the example. You may cry and complain about what people are saying and doing to you, but have you considered Jesus' ordeal and the weight of the cross that He had to bear? If you want to get over your pain and suffering, think about the terrible things Christ had to endure. You complain that people do not like you because of how you look, your size, or your neighborhood. Do you know that Jesus feels your pain? He ran His race with patience, although men set traps for Him and called Him evil names. He kept His eyes on what He had to gain.

You must shed the pounds of hurt and despair that have been placed in your life by people who care more about how you look than the depth of your character. The difference between you and Jesus is that He did not allow the preconceived thoughts of people to conquer Him. If He had, then our sins and their vast weight would have made it impossible for Him to hang on the cross. Think of all the people who will walk this earth, and then think about their sins that Jesus had to carry. Now, what if He would have let negative talk stop Him from carrying your sins to Calvary? Where would you be? Men prejudged Him and they will prejudge you just the same, but follow Christ's example all the way to the finish line.

Once you can see yourself through the eyes of God, shedding the weight will become that much easier. What people think of you will become less important because you will be losing those issues that caused you to pack on the spiritual pounds. Through God's eyes, you will see a person that has been healed from the humiliation and shame that had accumulated over the years that once made you hate who God had created you to be.

Jesus gladly carried the load for us. He knew that our shoulders were too weak to haul the issues that the world placed on us. God never meant for us to carry the feelings of inadequacy that we drag around from day to day. He wants to be our burden bearer, our heavy load carrier. All He wants is for us to put the issues that are too heavy for us to carry on His shoulders. Jesus' shoulders are strong enough to carry the weights that keep slowing us down and prevent us from reaching the finished line.

The devil knows that you are weak in the flesh without God. His job is to add pressure to your fragile ego until the weight of it pulls you down to where he is. If you do not free yourself from the negative images that you have of yourself, they will sink you quicker than quicksand. Learn now before it's too late because the Scriptures say, "*Satan hath desired to have you, that he may sift you as wheat*" (Luke 22:31 KJV). He knows you inside and out just as Jesus does, and he will do whatever it takes to break you into pieces and destroy you with your own mind. The mind determines how you see yourself—positively or negatively.

Overweight from a poor perception of self is just as unhealthy as being physically overweight. It will eventually cause serious health problems or eventually death. People are committing suicide because they are unable to cope with the pressure of not fitting into a certain image. Overindulging on their appearance is killing them emotionally as well as spiritually.

If you do not believe that your appearance can become a weight issue, just turn on your television and look at what is happening to the young stars that are under the scrutiny and watchful eye of the critics and tabloids. They are turning to alcohol, drugs, and dieting themselves until they are just skin and bones in an attempt to fit into the beautiful crowd. Not being able to maintain those standards is causing them to become overweight with issues that they are too young and immature to handle.

Young adults have difficulty just being themselves. They do not have to grow up so fast, but the career paths that many have chosen are telling them differently. Many careers put them in a position where they have to look like skeletons if they want to enjoy them for very long. Their bodies have not fully developed, yet they are hearing negative comments that they need to lose weight. This will cause them to starve their immature bodies into stick figures. Unfortunately, this is the life that they have chosen—a life that is killing them to be someone that God never meant for them to be.

Self Control

Being physically overweight begins when you overindulge with food. Being spiritually overweight begins when you overindulge on the negative comments that are said about you. Neither one is good for you. You must have the power within to have self-control over both. The more food you put into your stomach, the fuller it becomes and the more weight you gain. The more positive things that you put into your spirit man, the more it will increase your faith and cause the weight of negative thought to diminish. The apostle Paul tells us that every man is born with a measure of faith, but whether it's increased or not depends solely on you. The negative things that you hear about yourself are like eating junk food. The more you eat of them, the worse you feel.

If you increase your faith in what Christ has said that you are in Him, then you will feel the weight dropping off your body. Nothing happens overnight, but it takes encouraging yourself and believing God's Word that you are perfectly and wonderfully made in Him.

Paul talks about your spirit man being trained and fit just as you would

get your physical body trained for an Olympic race. When a runner pre-
pares for a race, he gets his body in tiptop shape. Excess weight will slow
him down over the course of the race. The same is true for the spiritual
body. Accumulated weight will slow you down if you have not conditioned
your spirit man to handle the putdowns and attacks while running life's
race. When you attempt to jump over the hurdles of depression and low
self-esteem, you are too exhausted from the weight to make it over because
you did not prepare yourself for these obstacles.

Some people will never understand why they cannot drop the pounds
of old issues. They continue to take in the wrong things that keep them
spiritually obese. You must be careful when eating from "Pharaoh's table"—
negative people. Sure, everything looks exquisite and tastes delicious, but
their aftereffects are what gets you. Before long, you will find yourself in a
spiritual rut, too heavy to move because of gluttony.

If you continue to eat from Pharaoh's table, sooner or later it will catch
up with you. You will find yourself not as spiritual as you once were. Every
negative force that comes against you seems to take you down a notch.
Because you failed to train the spirit, you kept eating the wrong things,
which have become stumbling blocks and weights in your life. Everything
seems to make you feel self-conscious, from the way that you look to the
decisions that you make in life. The hurtful comments that you once easily
ignored are affecting you now and causing you to look differently at yourself; even the way you talk makes you self-conscious. And to think that it
all started because you sat at the wrong table, overindulging on the wrong
cuisine.

Now you are all bent out of shape, depressed, and feeling bloated with
issues because you stopped exercising the spirit man and became a spiritual
coach potato—nursing the wounds of your bruised ego. Too lazy to get up
and do something about your weight problem, now you blame others for
your situation and lack of productivity.

How does a person keep from becoming spiritually obese when faced
with many of life's challenges? Start by building your faith in Christ so that
you will be spiritually fit to stand against the fiery darts aimed at you. Life
is like a race. It has three parts, the beginning, where everyone is excited
because they have conditioned their bodies for months to get prepared for
the race. All the runners have shed the extra pounds that may slow their
speed. Now they are prepared to show the crowd what they can do. In the

middle of the race, they begin to second-guess themselves and wonder if they are as good as they thought they were. They become tired and weary and want to give up once they see their opponents ahead. They are exhausted because they did not lose enough weight or prepare as diligently as they should have. At the end of the race, they can finally see the finish line. They begin to believe that they have a chance of winning, only to look back and see the heavy load dragging behind them.

God wants us to prepare our spiritual bodies just as strenuously as we would our physical bodies. Life is a race, and how well we prepare for it will protect us from those that speak damaging words that may keep us from making it to the finish line. If we do not exercise our spirit man and remove all the excess pounds, we will eventually fall by the wayside as we attempt to complete the laps set before us. Many start out strong, only to give up before the race official declares a winner. In a physical contest, there can only be one winner; but in the spiritual race there are many, because we each are striving towards the same goal. When we allow our minds to become crowded with past and present hurts, we fail to see ourselves victorious in the race. We rise and fall because of life's weights that keep dragging us back to the starting line.

Most people will gain excessive weight due to depression. They will eat and eat until one day they realize that the pounds have accumulated. The same is true in a mental sense. Once you allow Satan to show you that you have nothing to live for and that no one cares about you, the mental weight begins to stockpile. Satan put negative thoughts into your mind, making you believe that everyone is against you, when they are not.

> *For the weapons of our warfare are not carnal, but mighty through God to pulling down of strong holds; casting down imaginations, and every high thing that exalteth itself against the knowledge of God, and bringing into captivity every thought to the obedience of Christ* (2 Corinthians 10:4-5 KJV).

God has the power to put all of Satan's strongholds and vain imaginations into subjection. There is nothing that you cannot overcome, including the conquering of your weight. The weapons that Satan uses such as depression, vain imagination, and a poor self-image were defeated when Jesus went to Calvary and died, so that your weight issues can be obedient unto His voice and not Satan's.

People suffer each day from the pain and heartache that others have caused. Others suffer from the pain and heartache that they have brought upon themselves. No one has told them that they are unattractive or too fat; instead, it's the opposite. They get compliments from friends and family, but that termite—Satan—has made them believe otherwise. He is the one that has caused them to feel inferior and inadequate in their minds. The pressure to be perfect is devastating them.

Mental obesity is destroying millions each year just as physical obesity is. Mental obesity causes people to be preoccupied with issues that do not exist. Seeing how beautiful they truly are is difficult for them. The mirror shows them a perfectly acceptable image of themselves, while their mind sees something totally different. They feel the need to improve where none is needed.

Each day will be like taking baby steps when you are trying to rid yourself of excess weight. With Christ, you can overcome any tragedy such as molestation, rape, incest, physical and mental abuse, or inadequacy that has caused you to become spiritually obese throughout the years. You can conquer and jump over any hurdles that Satan has put before you. Reclaim your life today and watch the pounds—the negative images you had of yourself—melt away.

Chapter Fifteen

Behind These Eyes

Shall I look to the mountain gods for help? No! My help is from Jehovah who made the mountains! And the heavens too! He will never let me stumble, slip, or fall. For he is always watching, never sleeping. Jehovah himself is caring for you! He is your defender. He protects you day and night. He keeps you from all evil and preserves your life. He keeps his eye upon you as you come and go and always guards you (Psalms 121:1-8 TLB).

Kelvin was always the life of the party. If you wanted to have a good time, then he was the man to call. Kelvin had a bad case of acne, which made him feel unattractive, so he partied to the extreme to make people believe that he was secure in himself. But little did they know, Kelvin was hiding a secret. He was ashamed about how he looked. In his friends' eyes, all they saw was a man that lived life to the fullest. But inside, Kelvin was in pain and drowned his sorrows with drinking uncontrollably. He never told anyone how he really felt; therefore, he was left to suffer alone. Kelvin looked one way on the outside, but behind his eyes rested depression and shame.

All the trials and tribulations that you have endured in life have probably prompted you too to put up a wall of defense. God says that He keeps His eyes upon you as you come and go. He sees your pain when others do not, because His watchful eyes are constantly on you to protect you from slipping or falling prey to your circumstances. Although man can only see your outer appearance, God sees much deeper. He sees your tears in the midnight hour. He sees the inner torment and the punishment that you have placed upon yourself needlessly. He is always there to comfort and to keep you in perfect peace. He sees the forced smile that you wear to hide the pain of what is really going on inside of you.

God wants us to look towards the heavens where He is because He alone has the answers to our problems. He has been our defender and protector from the storms in our lives. He has guarded and kept us as we searched in vain for the answers to our happiness. Jesus is waiting on us to unlock the self-made prisons into which we have confined ourselves. He has given us the keys to freedom through His Word.

Many of us are living hypocritical lives. We want people to believe that our lives are perfect, and we assume a facade to camouflage the truth. We are living secret lives. What others see on the outside is not really who we are on the inside.

Have you ever found yourself considering thoughts similar to those described below?

If people truly knew the real me, they would see the pain that resides behind my lying eyes. No one knows the hurt and shame that I have endured over the years because I have managed to put on a big smile, pretending that everything is going great in my life. When people see me, they see perfection; but in reality, I feel as though my whole life is crumbling apart. Behind these eyes are self-hatred and years of hiding the truth from all those around me. If only they knew the real me. My friends think that because I can get what I want, I have it made. Little do they know that material possessions do not bring happiness. I make fun of people only to hide my insecurities. I do this because it helps me to forget what I think and feel about myself. Behind these eyes are hidden much heartache and confusion, so much so that I find difficulty in lifting my eyes to the hills from where my health and mental stability comes—God. My days seem like night and my nights seem unending because of the spiritual turmoil taking place and hindering me from seeing myself as Christ does.

People are fighting and wrestling within themselves because of the false image that they portray before others. They put on a show that everything is okay in their lives. In most situations, it's the person that appears to be the life of the party. When you look into their eyes, they appear so full of life and excitement, when in reality they are dealing with issues that no one ever imagined.

God does not want us to feel as though we have to carry our burdens alone. He is standing at the top of the mountain, waiting on us to take our minds off our situations and focus on Him. He is standing there with open arms telling us to cast our cares upon Him because He is able to carry what we cannot.

God wants us to know that life can be better if we would just realize that He is here for us. No amount of hurt or pain can overtake us if we look into His Word and see the plans that He has laid out for us. Through His Word, we are healed, delivered, and set free from the bondage of depression, low self-esteem, and feelings of unworthiness. He wants us to look towards the only hill that has the ability to set the captive free from all the demonic turmoil that is dwelling on the inside.

Only the true and living God has the power to set high and look low on those that are struggling with the issues of life. He knows the pain and suffering that are hidden behind their eyes. Although He has the power to remove the hurt, we have to want to be helped. It hurts God when He sees one of His children brokenhearted. The power has to come from within us to want to shed the misery that we have allowed Satan to bring into our lives. Yes, God has the power to take the pain away, but He does not force Himself on anyone. We have to want to be helped.

Wearing Masks

Can you image if we could see behind the eyes of those that have gone on killing rampages within our schools and our jobs? Just think about the ones that we could have stopped, if only we knew the hurt and pain that they had been carrying. However, we have become so preoccupied with our lives that we could not recognize when they were hurting. They left clues all around us, but we never noticed them because we were too busy to care or get involved. So, when we turned on our televisions, we saw the outcome of our lack of care.

We work, play, and attend church with people who wear masks portraying that everything is fine in their lives, but the truth behind their eyes and smiles tells a different story. Do we take the time to find out how their day is going or do we say, "I will ask the next time that I see them"? I know that I am guilty. On numerous occasions God has put it on my heart to call and to encourage someone; but instead of doing it when He tells me to, I let the day drag on and forget to do it. We all make excuses, but while doing so, someone may be contemplating suicide while we go about our busy schedules. At times, all a person really needs is to know that someone else is concerned about what we are going through; but as usual, our agenda takes precedence over their so-called minor problems, which have a way of turning into major ones.

For those of you that know people that have gone on killing sprees, have you ever asked yourself this question: *If I had taken the time to talk or befriended them, could I have been the one to have made a difference in the decision that they made?* Or, *Could I have led them to Christ or helped them to get some professional help?* Could you have been the one to prevent people from being gunned down on the school playground, the mall, or on your job? "If only" is often said after the fact. Don't become the next person to say, "If only."

> *The light of the body is the eye: if therefore thine eye be single, thy whole body shall be full of light. But if thine eye be evil, thy whole body shall be full of darkness. If therefore the light that is in thee be darkness, how great is that darkness!* (Matthew 6:22-23 KJV).

Jesus was letting His disciples know that if they were genuine, it would shine bright like a light through their eyes and people would see it. Many people can see straight through you and know if you are sincere just by looking into your eyes. When you have the right intentions and motives, people will see the sincerity in them. But if evil is in your heart, the eyes will possess a sinister and sneaky appearance. I have personally encountered people like this. No matter how nice they pretended to be, there was a coldness or darkness in the way they appeared.

Some people have found themselves like King David, asking God,

> *How long will you forget me, Lord? Forever? How long will you look the other way when I am in need? How long must I be hiding daily anguish in my heart? How long shall my enemy have the upper hand? Answer me, O Lord my God; give me light in my darkness lest I die. Don't let my enemies say, 'We have conquered him!' Don't let them gloat that I am down* (Psalms 13:1-4 TLB).

Behind those eyes is a person that feels defeated by those that seek to destroy him or her. That individual's hope and faith in life is fading, while his or her enemies are gloating over the pain that they have caused. It appears as though God does not hear this person's prayers, but He does. The grief and pain being experienced makes it seem that this person is fighting a losing battle. God knows that he or she has been wounded and is waiting on the individual to see past the smoke clouds so that He can bandage the wounds.

Maybe you can relate to the person I have described here. Although the eyes hide secrets, they will reveal how the enemy (Satan) has drained and worn a person down emotionally. The enemy is not always a stranger. You do not have to step outside your home to feel the sting from your enemies; many are living, sleeping, and breathing within your own home. Oftentimes, it's not the people that you do not know that seek to hurt you but the ones that you call your friend, mother, father, brother, or sister that look for ways to destroy your confidence in who you are as a person. They do it unintentionally and sometimes intentionally, which stems from the lack of confidence that they have in themselves.

Some people have prayed and asked God why they were born into a family that is cruel and has no regards for others' feelings. Rest assured that nothing gets past God. The Scriptures say, *"The eyes of the Lord . . . run to and fro throughout the whole earth"* (Zechariah 4:10 KJV). Yes, God sees the cruel treatment that is inflicted upon you. But if you know who you are as a child of God, it becomes easier over a period of time to handle. It's not that God turned His back on you, but He left Scriptures to teach you how to overcome the hurt and pain that you will face in this life.

No one but you has the power to pick yourself up and move on with your life. Stop giving your enemies the authority that God has given you. They use what you have told them about yourself against you. They beat you down with your own information. There is truth to the saying that "Loose lips sink ships." You lower yourself by exposing information that you should be talking to God about and not to others.

King David says, *"Even my best friend has turned against me—a man I completely trusted; how often we ate together"* (Psalms 41:9 TLB). Do not be dismayed when you find out that your so-called trusted friend was the one that stabbed you in the back. King David said that this was a man that he dined with and trusted with his life. When you are confident and happy in who you are, sometimes other people do not want to see you that way. They thrive on misery and want others to feel the same as they do. So wipe those tears from your eyes and pray to God to restore the joy and happiness that you once had. Never let anyone steal your joy—not even your closest friends because they will come and go. As God takes you to another level in your life, your true friends will be revealed. The very person that betrays you might be the one that you opened your home to and with whom you shared a meal. Do not be caught off guard when this happens.

Behind our eyes should be a person that is confident, happy, and free because of Jesus. We are not going through anything that He has not experienced. He knows what it feels like to be betrayed by friends and to be deserted by family. The difference between Jesus and us is that He knew who He was according to the Word of God. Men labeled Him as an outcast, crazy, and ignorant, but God said, *"This is my beloved Son, in whom I am well pleased"* (Matthew 3:17 KJV). Jesus made God proud of Him, because He did not care what men said or thought about Him. He cared only about pleasing His Father.

The next time someone looks into your eyes, let that person see a man or woman who is confident. If you decide to be the life of the party, let it be because you are secure in whom God created you to be and not to cover up your insecurities. Your acne, weight, or skin color does not define you, but every word that proceeds out of the mouth of God. Embrace who you are and live life to the fullest.

Chapter Sixteen

The Struggles From Within

Each day when I begin life's journey, I hide my fears, my tears, and my shame. No one knows how I really feel inside because everyone is too busy to notice. Over the years, people have torn me apart with their negative and insulting words. My concerns don't involve people outside of my family; for the most part, it's my family that is causing all the hurt that I am feeling. I thought that love was kind, but what they think is love is causing me to be in turmoil constantly with myself. Friends and family call it constructive criticism, but I call it verbal abuse.

The happiness that I displayed before the crowd was all a charade. I have learned how to fool people by keeping my feelings concealed. But what scares me the most is that one day all the abuse and criticism that I have taken from others will cause me to explode from tucking it inside for years. We do deceive; I am lying each day that I pretend to be confident and assured in myself, when actually I am one big train wreck waiting on someone to discover the crash and clean up the mess.

Some people would say that a person appearing normal on the outside can't be hiding deep, dark secrets, but they do each and every day. We see them as we go about our daily lives, never realizing what is going on in that person's life.

We all have insecurities and something to hide. Maybe it's the wife and mother that appears to have the perfect life but is hiding the fact that she uses drugs and alcohol to conceal the shame of living with an abusive husband. It could be the husband that goes to work each day to provide for his family, only to cover up his sexual addiction from those that know him as a stand-up citizen. Or maybe it's the high school student that seems to excel in academics as well as sports, only to hide that he or she has been molested by a family member or friend.

We all have something that we may carry on the inside. Those that are spiritual can see straight through us. The reason that many can't is that they are too busy to notice. When I was growing up, there was no way that we could hide our problems from the older generation. They would know that we were lying before we could open our mouths. Today's older generation teaches and preaches but often never reaches. Many more people today are dealing with low self-esteem and abuse right in their homes by their spouses, all the while displaying a masquerading smile that says everything is perfect in their lives.

We live in sad times, when people care more about a wounded animal on the streets than a wounded human that has been beaten and broken by life. We see activists on television protesting against inhumane treatment of animals, but we will keep silent when a child is being abused or when someone we know is on the verge of suicide, unable to cope with their problems. We often turn to look the other way. It is sad but true that we treat human life as worthless.

Lord, letting go of past hurts is not easy to do. How can I escape my past when others seem to throw it in my face constantly? It's not as if I do not want to let go and let God bring joy into my life. But how can I experience it when I am constantly being tormented by the bad memories of my past? When I feel that I have overcome a problem or an issue that I am dealing with, something else comes along that puts me back to square one.

I want to cry out to You, but will You hear me? Can you please stop the demonic spirits that are mentally tormenting me? I once was confident, but I allowed what others had to say tarnish the positive image that I had of myself. Their voices play over and over in my mind like that of a broken record, and now I second-guess the positive things that I once felt and knew about myself.

Now I realize that there was never anything wrong with me, because I can finally see that jealousy and envy were the motivating reasons for their lies. I have learned that my success and confidence made them ambush me with their negative comments. Nothing I ever did warranted such harsh treatment from them, but it was Your favor on me, Lord, that caused them to rise up against me.

I should have known that justice would soon prevail and that You would finally open my eyes to the truth before my enemies overtook me with their deception. Due to my vision being clouded, I could not see the beauty that You created in me—the caterpillar that was waiting to turn into a butterfly. Satan was trying to destroy all that he knew I was going to be.

I have shed many tears from the lies that I allowed others to feed me about myself, only to see that I am nothing like those untruths. I allowed myself to become depressed and oppressed trying to become someone that You never created me to be. The standards that I allowed others to force upon me, and the pressures that I placed upon myself to measure up to them, kept me feeling like a failure. Why can't people just allow me to find my way, instead of forcing their way of thinking upon me?

I thank you, Lord, for blessing me to finally see my inner beauty. The gossip and the slander against me no longer controls the way I see myself. I now know who You created me to be: strong, confident, and fearless.

Chapter Seventeen

Confessions of the Soul

Seeing people who are living tormented lives each day without anyone to care for them is disheartening. Why do we look down on people when all they want is help and to be accepted in this unacceptable society? We need to take a few minutes and listen to the people that come to us for advice or who just want to talk out their frustrations. They are crying out for our help. When talking with them, look them in their eyes, because they will tell the story as to what is really going on inside of that individual. Too often, we allow what is going on in our lives to overshadow everything else.

But thou, O Lord, art a shield for me; my glory, and the lifter up of mine head (Psalms 3:3 KJV).

Lift up your heads, O ye gates; and be ye lift, ye everlasting doors; and the King of glory shall come in (Psalms 24:7 KJV).

To You, O Lord, I pray. Don't fail me, Lord, for I am trusting you. Don't let my enemies succeed. Don't give them victory over me. None who have faith in God will ever be disgraced for trusting him. But all who harm the innocent shall be defeated. Show me the path where I should go, O Lord; point out the right road for me to walk. Lead me; teach me; for you are the God who gives me salvation. I have no hope except in you. Overlook my youthful sins, O Lord! Look at me instead through eyes of everlasting love and kindness (Psalms 25:1-7 TLB).

A defeated attitude keeps you from knowing the truth about God's love and kindness, the love that He wants to show you through His Word, and the mercy that He wants to pour on you when you make mistakes. God is saying, "Don't be so hard on yourself." You cannot be made whole when you have allowed Satan to weigh you down with his lies. God wants you to find the strength from inside to lift your head towards Him, so that you may be set free from the pressures of this life. When you smile, He wants it to be genuine and not masked by lies.

He wants you to confess to Him, because He's your help and the lifter of your head. God never meant for you to bow down and kneel to anyone, not even your circumstances. He wants you to know that the God that you serve has the power to take any tormenting spirits away, even those so-called friends and loved ones that wish to see you fail. Know that God has the power to sustain and keep you from their destructive path.

> *O Lord, so many are against me. So many seek to harm me. I have so many enemies. So many say that God will never help me. But Lord, you are my shield, my glory, and my only hope. You alone can lift my head, now bowed in shame. I cried out to the Lord, and he heard me from his Temple in Jerusalem. Then I lay down and slept in peace and woke up safely, for the Lord was watching over me. And now, although ten thousand enemies surround me on every side, I am not afraid* (Psalms 3:1-6 TLB).

King David wants us to know that he fought in the same battle that we are fighting today against Satan—not people. When a person tries to overcome a scandalous past, people that know of that scandal never let them forget it. Some people believe that God will not forgive them and feel hopeless; however, in Him there is hope and safety from those that have set out to destroy them with their yesterdays. God makes sure that we never have to miss a night of sleep worrying about the attacks from those that oppose us.

God is your shield; He is your lifter, your sustainer, and the reason for your hope. Yes, there may be pain hiding behind your eyes, and your head may be hanging low due to the ridicule from others. The God that you serve is able to put the twinkle back into your eyes and the rising of your head when others come to attack you. No other word has the power to deliver you like the Word of God.

If no one else notices your tears, rest assured that God does. His Kleenex is so wide that it's never oversaturated. So, wipe your weeping eyes because in God you will always have a shoulder to cry on and ears that will listen when you confess your troubles. Friends and family may laugh at you now, but God has a way of silencing those that come against you.

Satan knows that you are just a step away from your breakthrough. That is why he uses those that are closest to you to keep you filled with despair and hopelessness. He knows that if you ever see the path that God is trying to direct you towards, he will lose the battle of keeping you spiritually blind.

Being What God Intended

Life would be pleasant if people would not force others to live according to their standards of beauty. People put pressure on their kids, spouses, and friends to live up to what they think that they should be. The pressure causes individuals to become withdrawn and to become people that God never intended them to be. Therefore, they have learned how to mask their pain inside, pretending that their lives are perfect. King Solomon says, "*Laughter cannot mask a heavy heart. When the laughter ends, the grief remains*" (Proverbs 14:13 TLB). More energy is required to fake a laugh when your heart is breaking due to grief and pain.

When you are hurting from the inside but telling everyone around you that you are happy takes a great deal of effort. Usually no one ever suspected that anything was wrong with the people who end up committing suicide or walking into a building and taking the lives of others. They gave the appearance of happiness, and those around them believed that everything was okay in their lives, not realizing that behind their eyes and smiles was tremendous turmoil.

No matter how a person may laugh, how they truly feel will eventually surface. We must learn to be spiritually in tune with God's spirit so that we can see when a person is in trouble. We work and live around people that are hurting every day and never notice what is really going on. We need to learn to be very careful not to overlook clues from those that are seeking guidance. Those indicators may be the very ones that could have saved that person's life or kept him or her from making other bad decisions.

If you were the one who was suffering, wouldn't you want someone to be there for you and notice as well as acknowledge your pain? The friend that keeps bringing up how he or she feels wants to be acknowledged as well. Stop telling that person to get over it. It's not easy to get over a bad experience that has been embedded deep inside your soul.

Words Are Powerful

Words of a gossip are like choice morsels; they go down to a man's inner-most parts (Proverbs 18:8 NIV).

Words do hurt when they are said with malicious intent. They are felt in the very depths of a person's soul. The offended person may put on a brave face as if to say the distressing words were not taken to heart. Deep down inside, however, the thought that a person could say something so cruel brings pain and resentment.

In today's world, most people believe that they have the right to say whatever they want. But ask yourself, did your words have a part in the emotional damage of a brother or sister? Can you truly say no? Don't justify any potentially hurtful words by the fact that no one seemed to be bothered by them; pain caused by others is often hidden. We need to realize the full impact of our words; they can breathe life or death in a spiritual sense into another person's life. Words can be very dangerous when they are not used properly. We have all used words from time to time that have injured others emotionally and spiritually.

The Bible says, *"Death and life are in the power of the tongue"* (Proverbs 18:21 KJV), so if the words that I speak can bless or hinder my life, they can bless or hinder someone else's life as well. We usually know when we have hurt someone's feelings, but many of us have a problem with apologizing for fear that it makes us looks small and weak. Words have a way of destroying a person's self-perception. It's like a cancer that spreads until it deteriorates the entire body. We must let go of what was said about us, especially when the intent of the words was hateful.

Gossip has a way of making the person that is spreading the rumors feel important. It makes the individual feel that he or she has something important or worth telling about another. Not realizing that those words are like poisonous venom waiting to enable its victim, gossip makes the individual feel empowered over the other person.

King Solomon hit the nail on the head when he said that gossip goes to the inner parts of a man because the hurt that he or she has felt from malicious lies has a way of showing up in that person's behavior. Some of the things that you are dealing with in your adult life come from the gossip or lies that you tucked deep within your heart. Those bad memories will come back to haunt you when dealing with others.

Have you ever wondered why looking at your child or others around you sometimes triggers something painful that you kept hidden? The anger that you hid inside has come back to surface. The fake smile and happiness that you displayed to friends have come crashing down on you. Now you are taking all those years of hurt out on those closest to you because you never dealt with the negative words that were spoken against you.

Life is a like a circle; everything has a way of coming back around. Any lies that were told about you or the hurt that you now suppress will return to you. You must learn through the Word of God how to let go of your issues and release them to God before you allow them to destroy you and those around you.

Pay attention to how any demeaning or harsh words make your child feel. Just think about how it made you feel when others talked that way to you. All you have to do is look in that child eyes; they will give you your answer. Children are not as good as adults are at masking their feelings. They usually will act up in some way or the other. Most parents miss the clues because they are so wrapped up in their own issues that they cannot see the pain and suffering in their children.

We pass our dysfunctions onto our children. We see things in them that we thought could never exist. They have learned from us how to suppress their pain and feelings, but they act it out in other ways than we do. Many of our kids today have no conscience; they can take an animal and mangle it to death. We are breeding natural born killers because of the pain that they have tucked inside of them that no one—not even a parent—noticed. Something has gone terribly wrong inside our homes. As parents, we are working several jobs, leaving our babies to care for themselves. And when they need to talk with us, we are often too tired to listen. Follow the clues because our children are dropping them like breadcrumbs.

People today seem to be more concerned with preserving a tree or animal than preserving the life of a precious child from his or her emotional problems. On television, we love to see stories of mass destruction, rather than a community lending a helping hand in educating our children to be the best that they can be. The late Marvin Gaye said it best, "What's going on?" Have we become so cold and callous towards others that we are immune to their suffering? I encourage you to pay attention to the emotional needs of your coworkers, neighbors, children, and spouses. Let them know that you are trustworthy when they come to you to confess their innermost secrets.

When a man is gloomy, everything seems to go wrong; when he is cheerful, everything seems right! (Proverbs 15:15 TLB).

King Solomon was the wisest man that had ever lived. He possessed undeniable wisdom. He knew that when people are confident and happy, they feel that they can conquer the world, but when they are feeling empty and unsure of themselves, they can do nothing right.

God never meant for us to bury our pain deep inside of ourselves. The next time someone looks into our eyes, let them see God's light shining through them instead of despair and hopelessness. It's not His desire to see us suffer. Pray to Him and He will hear, but we must be ready to dump all of our negative spirits at His feet. When we fail to release them over to God, they will remain a stumbling block in our paths.

I agree with the saying, "Confession is good for the soul." I encourage you to talk to someone with whom you feel comfortable. And stop holding onto your pain. Let it go! Confess it so that you can be free to live a life without worrying what others think of you. First John 1:9 (KJV) says, *"If we confess our sins, he is faithful and just to forgive us our sins, and to cleanse us from all unrighteousness."* Truly, confession is good for the soul.

Chapter Eighteen

Generational Curses — Part 1

And as Jesus passed by, he saw a man which was blind from birth. And his disciples asked him, saying, Master, who did sin, this man or his parents, that he was born blind? (John 9:1-2 KJV).

Are we doomed to fail before we exit the womb? Are we held accountable for the sins of our parents, actions over which we had no control? Are there generational curses that God has passed on to future generation because of their rebellious forefathers?

Past generations believed that God's wrath can and will be passed on to their descendants, but that is not true. Every man is held accountable for his or her own sins. If you feel cursed and circumstances are not going quite right in your life, then it's a strong possibility that you are out of the will of God. No one—not family or friends—can cause God's wrath to come upon you. No bloodline or family tree can bring a life of curses upon you. When you live outside of the will of God, you leave no room for Him to bless you. God will not bless your mess. If everything you attempt to do goes wrong, then I suggest that you look at the way you are living, not at your family tree.

Satan may tell you that since your father is an alcoholic or drug addict, then that is what you will become. That is far from the truth according to the Word of God. Christ's blood has freed you from the bondage of sin. His blood now dwells in you since you have accepted His invitation of salvation.

Researchers say that certain types of diseases, such as heart disease and diabetes, are inherited. However, no diseases can be passed through your spiritual bloodline. Spiritual diseases are sins, anything that hinders you from doing what is right. For example, if your father is a womanizer and spends his money in a drunken brawl, that has nothing to do with you becoming one. If you choose to take this road like your father, it is a learned behavior, not a curse. No one can make you sin no more than anyone can make you live holy.

We all have behaviors that are learned. Some are good and others we need to unlearn because they are destroying our lives. We place the blame on our parents and others when our lives do not quite turn out the way that we plan. However, the decision to break the cycle of poverty, infidelity, and low self-image is up to us. We choose the person that we want to be, not our family heritage. I believe that people use the term "generational curse" as a crutch, especially when they do not want to be held accountable for their wrongdoings.

Jesus' disciples wanted to know whose sins caused the man to be blind—his or his parents'. People in the Bible days believed that if a child was born with a certain type of birth defect, someone in that bloodline obviously had sinned. But Jesus quickly dispelled their accusation by letting them know that neither this man nor his parents had sinned. His condition had been preordained in heaven for this appointed time to authenticate before men Jesus as the Messiah.

We must understand that those born with different types of deformities are not cursed, and God is not trying to teach someone in their family a lesson. That's life and we all will have our crosses to bear. We have no control over the way we are born. Most people learn to deal with it and move on with their lives, while others will blame someone else for their condition.

When we see someone with a deformity, we may instantly think that they come from a family that lived rebellious lives or that they had sinned, and now it's payback time from God. He does not have to destroy someone's life to get back at us. It is no one's fault when a loved one suffers from a debilitating illness. God has not cursed them. Both good and bad people must go through life's challenges. The key is that we cripple ourselves when we turn our afflictions into handicaps.

People have areas that are not quite as they would want in their families, but they make the best of their situations. Christ didn't complain to God about the family into which He chose for Him to be born. His was a family bloodline that was full of scandal. His ancestors were well known for prostitution, adultery, murder, poverty, and illiteracy. But Jesus kept His mind on the man that He would eventually become and not the circumstances surrounding His family tree. Jesus did not use the excuse that it was a generational curse that caused Him to be mistreated because of what happened to His ancestors throughout biblical history. He knew that His family lineage made Him worthy to be used to redeem man back to God.

We sometimes become depressed when we look at the family that we are born into and find ourselves asking God why. But know this: God does not make mistakes. He gave us the will of survival. Many gifted and talented people have come from parents that are hooked on drugs, alcohol, and prostitution. They rose above their families' bad names and faults. They did not allow the bad habits of their families to overshadow their dreams to succeed. At times, we fail in life because we can never let go—in our opinion—of being born into the wrong family. We become bitter, hateful, and depressed when we never look beyond our family shame. What we should ask ourselves is what do we consider the wrong family? Many people are born into families that possess great wealth and fame but wish that they had parents that were there for them, instead of shipping them off to boarding schools. Before we begin to think that we have it so bad, there are plenty of people who wish that they were in our shoes. Money and having everything at our fingers tips does not constitute happiness.

How is it possible for you to get past the scandal and shame that has happened in your family? Put your trust in God; believe who He says you are. Never let the families that you are born into define the person that God has created you to be. No so-called curse from your family can keep the blessings of the Lord from you when you chose to follow His way instead of the wickedness of your family. A family history of drug use does not determine that you will repeat the cycle. If for some reason you become hooked on drugs, you did it because that is what you chose to do. It was not a family curse or a generational curse; it happened because you did it to yourself. God has given each human being the gift of free will, so when you sniffed, shot up, or digested drugs, you made that decision. While some people are coerced by others to do drugs, the decision was still theirs to make.

We all have excuses as to why we turn out the way we do. I never met my dad until I was fourteen years old. He never tried to build a relationship with me. Now, I could have taken that experience and become bitter and hateful towards him, but I chose to do the opposite. I worked diligently at being the best person that I could be. I knew that I was a good kid. I was raised to have morals and values, regardless of not having him in my life. Now I won't lie. At first I thought that once I contacted him, he would be happy to get to know me, but it was not so. As a child, that rejection hurt me to my soul; but later in life, I rose above it. I felt that it was his loss. I had to realize that without him I had accomplished so much in my life, and that helped me to see that I had succeeded without him. How can I be cursed by not having a deadbeat dad in my life, when God has blessed me with so much? He has blessed me with many gifts and talents. Having an absentee dad did not cause me to turn to a life of crime, drugs, or depression. In fact, I thank him because this circumstance helped me to become a strong woman in the Lord. It also helped me to see and believe that I can do all things through Christ.

If a curse can be passed through generations, then that means that it cannot be broken. Tell that to the millions of successful people who became doctors, lawyers, businessmen and women, or professional athletes. If people were cursed before birth, how could they overcome poverty and adverse situations to become someone great in this society? Just ask Oprah Winfrey how she rose above poverty and sexual abuse to become one of the most powerful women in the world. So you see, there is no curse—only a false excuse for not living up to your potential.

A negative outlook on your surroundings allows you to see only the bad, without ever noticing the good. I know people that have everything going for them—on the surface—and yet are unhappy because of what happened in their childhood or they are ashamed of their roots. No matter how successful they become, they never get over their previous misfortune. When you focus on the past, you will never see the great future that God has in store for you. If all the great men and women that have shaped our world would have let their family circumstances determined their future, we wouldn't be where we are today as a nation. If they had allowed poverty to shape their future, they would have never known how their lives would have impacted our world today.

I believe that it takes faith and determination to pull oneself out of a bad living condition. When I occasionally sit and watch a football game with my husband, I notice that many of the players have unfortunate stories, but they persevered through tragedy to become the great players that they are. Many of them would have never gone to college if it weren't for sports that provided the avenue to their future. Before we become dissatisfied and bitter with our lives and want to blame a curse from our forefathers and mothers for our failures, look and see what you can do to rise above your family tragedies and failures to break the cycle. Make your family what you want it to be and don't build it on the past. It takes only one person's determination in a family to break the cycle of adverse conditions such as poverty, depression, or dying of preventable diseases.

In families with high teenage pregnancies and multiple baby daddies, the cycle can be broken and has been broken in many families. If you are a female and all you have seen in your family is underage pregnancies from your mother, grandmother, and great-grandmother, know that it can end with you. But you must be willing to take a stand against it. You must believe first that you are worth more in the eyes of God. You must stop listening to the lies from men or young boys that tell you what you want to hear. They take your most precious gift and move on to the next naïve female.

Men, you have the power through Christ Jesus to be the man of integrity that He has created you to be. God will show you that you can be a man without planting your seeds all across town. It's up to you to be a man that will be there for his family and be loyal to the person that God has given you. So you see, no generational curses exist. If your papa was a rolling stone, that doesn't mean that you have to choose to be one. God allows you to make the choices that you want for your life.

If your mother is an unfit mother, you do not have to become like her. You can become the woman that God wants you to be. Everything in life is a choice. You choose to be a prostitute, a deadbeat dad, an illiterate, an abusive parent, an alcoholic, or a drug addict. Your family tree did not do this to you. A learned behavior did this to you. Look around you; numerous men and women did not allow their family lifestyles to deter them from becoming physicians, nurses, scientists, or entertainers. The ball is in your corner; take it, run with it, and discover the person that God has created you to be.

Although we all have family members that we wish we could lock in a closet and throw away the key, Christ knew who and what family to which He wanted each of us to belong. Some people in our families may be loud and embarrassing, drunks, drug addicts, molesters, thieves, or compulsive liars; but they do not define us. They chose to live these types of lives. No curse from the dark side did these things to them. However, when we remove ourselves out of the will of God, we open the doors for anything to happen to us.

Making a Great Future

For those like me that grew up without a birth father taking part in their lives, we can do something about it when we decide to have children. Be there for them and even if there is a divorce, continue to be in the lives of your children. Divorce does not mean that we have to play the disappearing act in their lives like our fathers or mothers have done with us.

Take the loss of your absentee father or mother, and the pain that it caused, and turn it into something positive in your life. Most young girls that grew up without a positive male role model in their lives often turn to older men for the love that they did not receive from their fathers. I thank God that I did not take that route. I knew that not having my birth father in my life did not mean that something was wrong with me but that something was wrong with him. He is the one that has the problem, but most young girls and boys never come to that reality. They grow up bitter and angry. They blame their mother for the father being absent in their lives, but if your dad wanted you in his life, wild animals could not keep him away from you.

So stop blaming others and move on to the great future that God has planned for you. Think about how awesome you will be as a parent. See yourself as God does, and you will be able to come through any bad situation as pure gold. If you need an example of a father figure, look to God to guide and order your steps. If you did not have a positive image of a father growing up, just think about how God has been there for you before you were conceived. Pray to Him that He will show you how a real woman or man should raise their children because He brought His children, the Israelites, from bondage to freedom.

God Gives Us a Way Out

People try to justify their wrongdoings by referring to a generational curse on their lives. They use the Old Testament to try and validate their claims. But, they make these claims in vain because God always gives us a way out of our sinful lifestyles. Exodus 20:4-6 (TLB) says,

You shall not make yourselves any idols . . . You must never bow or worship it in any way; for I, the Lord your God, am very possessive. I will not share your affection with any other god! And when I punish people for their sins, the punishment continues upon the children, grandchildren, and great-grandchildren of those who hate me, but I lavish my love upon thousands of those who love me and obey my commandments.

We misinterpret these Scriptures when we want to justify why things are not going well in our lives. The children, grandchildren, and great-grandchildren that God speaks of are those that are disobedient to the Word of God. They are following in their ancestors' footsteps. If any sinners' descendents believe, trust, and live by God's words, they will be blessed (they shall live and not die). The Bible tells of evil kings that had offspring who chose to follow the laws of God and were not cursed for the wickedness of their fathers. On the other hand, there were kings and prophets that followed God's way, but their children did not. We must understand that God never intervenes with our free will, which makes humans unique. There are other Scriptures that expose the myth of generational curses:

The one who sins is the one who dies. The son shall not be punished for his father's sins, nor the father for his son's. The righteous person will be rewarded for his own goodness and the wicked person for his wickedness. But if a wicked person turns away from all his sins and begins to obey my laws and do what is just and right, he shall surely live and not die. All his past sins will be forgotten, and he shall live because of his goodness. "Do you think I like to see the wicked die?" asks the Lord. "Of course not! I only want him to turn from his wicked ways and live" (Ezekiel 18:20-23 TLB).

If everything you do or touch seems cursed, it would be wise for you to look at how you are living according to the Word of God. God will not tolerate evil in His sight, and it will be punished. The tragedy comes when kids mimic what they see their parents do and even follow in their lives of sin. A child believes that whatever his or her parents do must be right. This is the behavior that causes a person's seed to be cursed because they follow in his or her footsteps of sin. Not only has that person gone astray, but also the gift of a child that God has blessed the parent with has been misguided to believe that the evil lifestyle of the parent is acceptable. The curse comes when a person decides that God's way seems unholy, and then it is passed on to the next generation when that person refuses to break the cycle of rebellion against God. God is love, and it's His desire that none should perish but have everlasting life. You choose your fate. No one has the power to curse you but you.

The children of Israel chose the life they wanted to live when they decided to rebel against God. He set rules and boundaries that would keep them undefiled and holy, but the enticement of sin lured them into a cursed life. Four hundred years went by after the book of Malachi was written. The children of Israel had been in bondage to foreign countries. They had lost numerous battles when they rebelled against God. Many of their men, women, and children were slaughtered or taken captive. Their homes were burned and possession taken. God shut up the windows of heaven, or blessings, to His people because they refused to follow His commandments. However, there was a remnant of people that stood, believed, and had faith in the promises of God. He heard their cries and sent His Son into the world that they might live and not die.

No matter what your family history may be, know that your heritage does not define you. Today is the day that you stop blaming past generations for your misfortunes. The power of life and death is in your tongue to speak success into your life. You have the power to stay crippled or to rise up to be whatever you set your mind to be. The ball is your court; what you decide to do with it is up to you, but just know that history doesn't have to repeat itself. You can change it for the better.

Chapter Nineteen

Generational Curses — Part 2

King David was a man after God's own heart, but his son Absalom was evil and rose up an army to kill him (see 2 Samuel). Samuel was God's anointed priest, but both his sons were evil (see 1 Samuel 8). Other evil people are described in the Bible, but in some cases, someone in their family eventually decided to follow the way of the Lord. Your family bloodline does not curse you. You can be born into a house full of sinners and be the one that preaches the Word of God to them. If there were such a thing as a generational curse, how could God use a prostitute, Rahab, to protect the spies? (see Joshua 2).

That very prostitute was in the bloodline that our Lord and Savior Jesus Christ would come through generations later. Rahab changed the course of her fate and family when she decided to risk her life to save the men of God. In turn, God spared her life and her entire household from a life of destruction.

We need to shake those rotten apples off our family tree. We do not have to be a product of our ancestors. It's just like saying, "Nobody ever amounted to anything in my family, so I guess I won't either." That is one of the silliest things that we could ever allow to roll off our tongues. Being born into poverty does not have to shape anyone as long they see themselves through the eyes of God. If a generational curse existed, why would God use the children that had parents with scandalous backgrounds to preach and proclaim His Word? Jesus says that He came to set the captives free, so if your family tree has you held captive to sin, God has given you the ability to break free. A family curse has no dominion over those that follow the will of God. In Matthew 5:17 (KJV) Jesus says, *"Think not that I am come to destroy the law, or the prophets: I am not come to destroy it, but to fulfil."* The curse was disobedience, not our family lineage. If we were a cursed generation, why would God waste His time sending His Son to a world that was doomed from the start? This would mean that Christ died in vain, since there would be no hope. If a curse were on our lives, why would God call us a royal priesthood? (see 1 Peter 2:9).

You have the ability to shape your future through Jesus Christ. No man has the ability to curse what God has blessed and ordained. He has set you apart for His glory, and this glory is determined by how you break free from your family cycle of sin. Yes, it's true that all have sinned, but God is talking about the practice of sin. *"For all have sinned, and come short of the glory of God"* (Romans 3:23 KJV). If you commit adultery and continue indulging in this illicit act, it becomes a habit and you are practicing and living in continual sin. This is what brings on the curse in your life; it only becomes generational when the cycle is not broken. But that does not mean that it cannot be stopped. It stops when you begin living right in the sight of the Lord.

Theologians speculate that Mary Magdalene was a prostitute, but what we do know for certain is that she later was a follower of Christ. Paul was a chief prosecutor of the church, but God used him to proclaim the same Word that he had once condemned. If you feel unworthy of the blessings of the Lord, hold your head up high and know that your family's indiscretions do not shape your future. God allows you to determine whether or not you want to be cursed; if you want to live a life that is filled with sin, then that is your choice.

Crime and Punishment

Israel was 100 percent at fault for the troubles that came upon them. God did not turn His back on them; they turned their backs on Him and His way of holiness. The curse or punishment came upon anyone that stepped outside of the will of God. The Mosaic Law had guidelines for Israel to follow. God refused to allow them to abuse and take advantage of each other and live lives that would cause other nations to see His people in disgrace. How would it look if God allowed them to live in sin as the surrounding countries watched and laughed with disgust? Their enemies would say, "These are the people that God has called 'chosen,' and yet they live lives that disrespect Him."

The curse was upon anyone that fell outside of the will of God. True, the Scripture does say that the curse will be upon Israel in future generations, *". . .visiting the iniquity of the fathers upon the children unto the third and fourth generation of them that hate me; and shewing mercy unto thousands of them that love me, and keep my commandments"* (Exodus 20:5-6 KJV). The conjunction *but* is what makes the difference in this sentence. The curse was upon anyone that rejected the Lord as his or her God. Mary, the mother of Jesus, was included in Israel's bloodline, but God sent His precious Son to be born into the world through her despite Israel's sins. Mary's lifestyle found favor with God. She lived a life that was pleasing in the sight of the Father. Why did God find favor in so many future Israelites, instead of plaguing them with a dreaded curse? Galatians 3:13 says, *"Cursed is every one that hangeth on a tree,"* meaning that Jesus became the curse for all on Calvary's Hill. Everyone has to stand on his or her two feet and give an account of the sins that he or she has committed. Jesus became sin that we may be forgiven when we fall short of God's glory.

The term *generational curse* cannot be found in the Bible. I believe that men came up with this to justify their failures in order to have something or someone to put the blame on when things in their life did not work out the way they think that they should. Why would God waste His time cursing someone for something that others are responsible for committing? When God created man, He put a part of Himself in him. People curse themselves when they walk contrary to God's Word. No one is born a failure; you become what you believe you are. The Bible says that death and life are in the power of the tongue. Whatever you say you are is what you will become. No one has the power to destroy your future but you. I do not believe that a Holy God would say in His Word that you could have whatever you say (when you are in His will) and then curse you for someone else's sins.

When the Babylonians took Israel captive, God gave them many chances to repent and get back into His will, but they refused. So you see, you can choose to be cut off from the promises of God. No one can take the inheritance that God has given you through His Son. When you allow the devil to deceive you that God is trying to keep you from that blessing, you begin to accept what he is saying; and trouble find its way into your life. The devil wants you to believe the lie of a generational curse. He wants you to believe that you will be a failure just like your father and that you will never amount to anything. But, God's Word tells a different story. You are the way that you are because you are not willing to live right before God.

A bastard shall not enter into the congregation of the Lord; even to his tenth generation shall he not enter into the congregation of the Lord (Deuteronomy 23:2 KJV).

Everything that God does has a spiritual meaning behind it. Deuteronomy 23 offers many regulations that Israel had to follow, not because they were considered better than other nations, but because God did not want them to become spiritually defiled by the sinful lifestyles of others. Deuteronomy had guidelines that Israel had to abide by if they were to stay morally clean in the sight of God. The same is true for generations today. If you allow spiritual garbage to pollute your mind, you will become a bastard child in God's sight. This word means that you prefer to follow the examples of the world and give no thought to what God says about living spiritually pure. Sin separates you from Him, and if you are not a child of God, that makes you illegitimate.

There are countless numbers of illegitimate children walking in darkness (sin). God did not make them that way, but they disowned Him as their Father and guiding force for their lives. When I was a child, I remember hearing adults using the words "bastard child." I understood that description to mean that a person that was born out of wedlock was doomed to hell. Those adults believed that if your parents were not married, then the child was damned. At the time, I thought to myself how useless it would be to try to live right if you were going to go to hell anyway. I believed that it was not fair for God to condemn someone for something over which he or she had no control. How can a child be responsible for entering into the world outside of wedlock? Why it is the child's fault for what two adults did? But thank God, as I grew up and began to be enlightened by His Holy Word, He showed me that a bastard child meant anyone that walked away from Him as his or her spiritual parent. These were rebellious children that love living in sin and refuse to turn from their wicked ways.

Before you take what someone has to say about your life to heart, I encourage you to search the Scriptures and see the plans that God has for your life. Your future is brighter than you know. Some people are only trying to find loopholes to cover up their shortcomings.

The Report of the Lord

Do you believe that you are part of a generational curse, or are you willing to believe the report of the Lord? Today is the day for you to see yourself as God does. Do not allow anyone to tell you whom you can or cannot be. Search the Scriptures; if you desire to be a lawyer, a doctor, a teacher, or a preacher, God has the ability to answer prayers. Even if those dreams do not come to pass, keep dreaming and believing that God has something bigger in mind for your life.

God has the power to bring those dreams to pass, but at times, it's your lack of faith that is keeping you from achieving them. You fail because you prefer to listen to people that were placed in your life by Satan to keep you defeated and depressed. Satan knows what is behind the doors that God wants to open for you. God is waiting on your faith to increase and for you to believe the impossible. God never opens a door for anyone that does not want it to be open.

It's time for you to know who you are in the Father. Stop listening to negative people that say it cannot be done. And stop focusing on the neighborhood in which you were raised. You can do and be anyone you want to be. But first, you must believe. It's not enough to see it in the Scriptures. You must believe through faith in those printed words that God created you to be victorious over every situation in your life.

How do you see yourself? Are you the head when it comes to over-coming obstacles in your life? Or are you the type of person when things do not work out that gives up and never tries again? One thing I love about Jesus, He never used what was not available. Everyone that was used in the Bible was doing something, whether it was good or bad.

Stop measuring or comparing yourself to others. God gave you the right stuff; use it! You are clothed in His spirit and washed in His blood. People focus on what they do not have instead of what they do have. So, when things do not work out in their lives, the first thing they want to say is, "It must be a generational curse." A curse has nothing to do with you not believing and succeeding in the plans that God has laid out for you. The problems come when you try to turn someone else's plans into yours. God never meant for you to be and do the same thing as everyone else. Many people are unhappy with the gifts and talents with which God has blessed them. They are too busy desiring the gifts that God has given to someone else. Learn to love and appreciate what God has given you. There are no big *I*'s or little *U*'s with God.

After reading this chapter, do you still believe that generational curses exist? We know now that they don't. When the disciple asked Jesus about the man that had been blind since birth, He made it clear that no one was to blame for this man's affliction. The situation at hand was for the Son of man to be glorified through the healing of the blind man.

So, take a closer look at your life and the family that Christ chose for you. You may be the one that He is going to use to change your family's future. God has the ability to use you and your determination to succeed in order to show someone that his or her life can be blessed too. The time is now to stop allowing where you come from or your parent's background to hinder you from receiving the promises of God. Know that no one has the power to stop you but you.

Rise above your family history because people need to see that God blesses those who have faith and are willing to live by the whole gospel and not by half. Your family tree does not determine the type of fruit that you will produce in your life. Every word that proceeded out of the mouth of the Lord controls your destiny.

Remember, you are not your mother or father. You are you! My encouragement is that you read God's Word and know that you are destined to succeed. You are not bound by the sins of the past but set free by the possibilities of your future.

Chapter Twenty

Too Beautiful for Words

Woe to the man who fights with his Creator. Does the pot argue with its
maker? Does the clay dispute with him who forms it, saying, "Stop,
you're doing it wrong!" or the pot exclaim, "How clumsy can you be!"
Woe to the baby just being born who squalls to his father and mother,
"Why have you produced me? Can't you do anything right at all?"
(Isaiah 45:9-10 TLB).

Kimberly Smith believed that she would be more beautiful if she lost
the excess weight, got a nose job, and added Botox to her lips to make
them bigger and to her forehead to remove the wrinkles. She achieved her
goal, only to find other things that she wanted to change about her appearance. This continued until she realized that she was gorgeous just the way
she was before all the surgeries. But now she looked unnatural and the
damage was permanent. Kimberly wished that she could undo years of
plastic surgeries after realizing that she was beautiful from the start.

What gives a man or woman the right to complain about the way that
God has made him or her? Why do we feel that He has made a mistake
when we do not look like everyone else? Did God's hands slip when He
put the final touches on us? When we look into our mirrors, the first features we point out are our flaws. Why can't we see the beautiful creation of
God? Why do we see the negative instead of the positive when looking at
our genetic makeup?

Isaiah made a valid point when he asked, "Does the pot argue with its
maker?" When beautiful antiques are being made, they never ask the artist,
"Why are you painting me this color?" They just sit on the shelves, while

people walk by and admire their beauty. But, we as humans are so critical to the point that we become angry with God about the way He designed us. Rick Warren, the author of *The Purpose Driven Life* says, "Anytime you reject any part of yourself, you are rejecting God's wisdom and sovereignty in creating you."

Isaiah went further to say, *"Woe to the baby just being born who squalls to his father and mother, 'Why have you produced me?'"* Many of us blame our parents for the way we turned out and have the audacity to say that we wish we had never been born. What makes a person look into a mirror and become depressed at the image that is staring back at them?

When we fail to believe and see that our Creator has made us wonderfully and beautifully correct, Satan has succeeded in blinding us of our true image. He is like the trick mirrors that we see at the amusement parks. The mirrors are only an illusion. When we stand in front of them, though, we believe the images that we see staring back at us.

You can cry and blame your parents for your physical features, but God had a design with you in mind. If you have the audacity to ask your parents, "Can you do anything right?" that is like finding fault with God. When you can see past what man says is beautiful, then and only then will you know that you are too beautiful for words.

To appoint unto them that mourn in Zion, to give them beauty for ashes, the oil my joy for mourning, the garment of praises for the spirit of heaviness; that they might be called trees of righteousness, the planting of the Lord, that he might be glorified (Isaiah 61:3 KJV).

God's Beautiful Creation

The creation of God is so beautiful that words cannot describe it. Just look at the lilies that grow in the fields. Who could have created a vision as beautiful as that? Or when the seasons change and everything appears new, giving yet another chance to reproduce all over again. Who but God could have created or thought to give life yet another chance to renew itself? Only He has the power to bring what was once withered and dead back to life. If God can renew and replenish the earth, surely He has the ability to renew the way you think about yourself.

Look into God's spiritual mirror. He took someone that was once beaten and battered by the hurtful words of others and transformed them

118

into the most beautiful creature walking on the earth. When you see your reflection, there are no words to describe the image that is staring back at you. God has given you beauty for ashes. Your former self has been burned and tossed into the wind when you finally see yourself through the eyes of God. In your mirror, you see a person that once lacked confidence. You once thought that you were not good enough according to man's standards. The ashes that you have traded in for beauty represent a person that knows now that his or her life matters. When you discover who you were created to be in Christ, you found the beauty that was lying beneath the rubble. The debris that you were buried underneath for years can now be removed because the ashes have been blown away to uncover the beauty that was there all along.

Too beautiful for words is what God thought when He designed every inch of our bodies. He loves every mole, stray hair, and extra layer of skin on our bodies. These are the parts that we hate about ourselves, but God loves our flaws. He has turned the things that we thought were ugly (ashes) into beauty. He made sure that there were no two humans alike—not even twins. Who else could make that claim except for God?

God has replaced your mourning with joy. No longer do you have to walk around feeling insecure. Your sorrow has been replaced with joy. You finally realized what God wanted you to see:

- You are beautiful just the way you are.
- Living in another's shadow will keep the real you from being seen.
- Joy will come when you stop complaining about what's wrong and embrace your individuality.

Too often, self-help books tell us to keep focusing on the positive things about ourselves, which is fine and good. But God wants us to do more. He wants us to mix those words with faith so that they can become a reality to us. We all have read books that have inspired us while reading them. But when we are finished, they become part of the book collection on our bookshelves. What happened to all that excitement and life changing words that we read? They never became reality to us. Therefore, we fell back into the same old rut. Those words were not mixed with faith; and without faith, we are unable to see ourselves as God does.

No, it's not enough to walk around quoting different sayings that talk about your self-worth and inner and outer beauty if you are never going to believe it. Why read God's Holy Word that talks about your worth to Him if you are not going to see yourself any differently? God is whispering in His soft voice that He wants to turn your pain into joy. He wants you to be self-assured in the person that He has created you to be. This will only happen if you take the time to see that many of your heartaches can be avoided if you will overcome your insecurities.

God wants to clothe you in His garment of praise to protect you from the spirit of heaviness, but self-pity is hindering you. The more you consume yourself with gloom and doom, the heavier you will become. God has told you on many occasions to rise up from your misery, but you have allowed your circumstances to burden you. Why is it so hard for you to believe that God created you beautiful? Your godly characteristics are what makes you beautiful. No words can explain the way that God sculpted you into existence. Men are baffled and stumble over their thoughts when they try to explain how God performed plastic surgery before there was such a surgery and how He used His hands to chisel man into the perfect species without making any mistakes.

We need to praise God for such awesome and breathtaking work because He has clothed us in His love. When the enemy comes to plant the seed of unattractiveness in us, we must learn to open our mouths and tell him that God says we are wonderfully and perfectly made. We should also tell the devil that we were made in God's image and washed in His Son's blood. He has equipped us with His characteristics, and because we are like our Creator, nothing about Him is ugly or distorted.

God has clothed you in Him that He may be glorified through you. When the enemy sees your confidence and that you know who you are in Christ, God gets the glory. He wants you to be victorious in Him and not listen to the lies of others. No one can make you feel unattractive or unworthy but you. When you allow hurtful words to penetrate through your secret place—the heart—self-doubt will form. Know that God does not create anything that is unattractive. It all started when man tried to tamper with God's creation. The double standards began and people were put into different classes of beauty and self-worth, when in fact God said all things that He made were good.

We all have some type of deep-rooted hang-ups about each other that must be resolved. If we close our hearts and minds to those that are different, then we will fail to see the beauty of God in them. God made it so that every race was carefully sculpted, and He put His final and best touches on us all—His Spirit. When we look at each other, we should point out our unique qualities; instead, we often think about what is wrong with the other person.

It is amazing how God made the human eyes. Some are slanted, some oval, and some wide. He varied the colors of our skin: black, brown, and white. No human can make claims to creating any of these beautiful features except for God. Sure, man can try it through plastic surgery. However, many that have undergone various procedures are displeased with the outcome.

Outside Influences

Can you imagine if you spent all your life being comfortable in your own skin, until you meet someone that tells you differently? You were fine until you allowed their negative aura into your life. Why do we allow others to enter into our lives and strip us of our identity? Why do we give them power over our lives? Satan has placed them in our lives to make us feel unloved, unwanted, and unattractive. We all wish that we could put the person that is hurting us in our position or shoes. We want them to know how it feels to be put down by negative comments.

If people could only know how their insults and name calling destroys how a person sees themselves. If you loved everything about me when we first met, then what has changed? Am I not the same person that you once loved and thought was the most beautiful person that you ever saw? What has changed in the relationship?

You need to know that it's not you who has changed or who did anything wrong in the relationship. Insecure people do and say hurtful things to make others feel as they do. When people are secure and confident, they hang around those that are the same. When people are not happy on the inside and are feeling unattractive and depressed about their appearance or lives, watch them. They will begin picking negative things out about you and say things that they think will hurt and make you feel the same as they do.

Pay attention to what a person is saying before you allow his or her negativity enter into your life and destroy the confidence that you have. Satan knows where your inner beauty originates. He speaks to your thoughts to make you second-guess what God has placed inside of you. Many have grown up hearing their parents or family member tell them how beautiful they are. But after they grew up and left the protection of their family, they met people with their own personal issues that tell them the opposite.

Our young girls are plagued with these issues as they mature into adulthood. They grow up feeling pretty and confident about themselves because their fathers reinforced it in them. But at some point in their lives, they meet young men who have been beaten down by life and had no positive family structure to influence them. They bring their low self-esteem issues into these young women's lives and destroy everything that the girls' fathers have built in them causing our young girls to become insecure. These girls feel ugly on the inside and out because they have allowed someone else to feed them lies about themselves. This someone has made them forget the confidence that was instilled in them from their youth.

Why do young girls allow this to happen to them—for love and acceptance? When you listen to negative words long enough, you will begin believing what you hear. Spoken words are a powerful force, because they have the ability to destroy you if you are mentally weak. Words go to the innermost parts of your soul. They can be positive or negative when spoken in a certain tone. Jesus proved this point when it came to salvation as well. It's not what you see that saves you but what you hear.

When you hang around people with nasty and mean personalities, those traits will eventually rub off on you. Young girls, for the most part, grow up believing and thinking that they can change the men that they love and don't realize that they will be the ones that end up hurt because God is the only one that has the ability to change a person. Nagging will eventually cause the man physically or verbally to harm the woman. When it's over, the woman will have lost herself trying to change someone that doesn't want to be changed. Therefore, she will end up losing her identity and the values that her parents instilled in her.

We may say that this could never happen to us, but love is a powerful addiction. If we get into a relationship without knowing who we are or who the other person is, getting caught into love's obsession trap will be easy. Just think about it. The apostle Paul told us that love would be the only thing that will stand in the end (see 1 Corinthians 13). So, love has to be a powerful force if it's the only thing that will last through the end of time. It is important to know whom we connect ourselves with when getting into a relationship. Not only can love be a good practice, it can also be one of the most dangerous and deadly obsessions. We should know our mate's mental stability because it can mean the difference between life and death.

Many women and men have become trapped in obsessive relationships by not getting to know their mates before the relationship became intimate. The obsessive person will break the weaker one down emotionally and mentally, especially when that individual knows that the other person's self-esteem is low. To keep you under their control, people like this will tell you how nobody else will want you because of your physical appearance or ignorance. They will constantly make up imaginary flaws that keep you in their power. They dominate the relationship to make you feel inferior just as someone in their past made them feel. Maybe it was their parents or a close family member that put them in an inferior environment. The reality is that each year women will lose their lives in abusive and obsessive relationships.

Looks can easily be deceiving. The beauty that God speaks about comes from within and manifests itself on the outward being. If you do not believe that you are beautiful, no one else can make you believe it. It cannot be found in a bottle, a pill, cream, or voices of others telling you so. True beauty comes when the Spirit of the Lord lives inside of you. No one can deny when that person sees the glow of the Lord resting upon you.

No matter how you try to change your appearance to please others, you will not be happy. Instead of changing the person God created you to be, you should change the people around you. Altering your appearance for others will become a continuous job because there will always be something that others will not like about you.

We all can find areas that we want to change about our bodies; but for most, it's not that big of a deal. There are plus-sized women that love the way God created their bodies. They flaunt it on magazines covers, television, and on the runways as models. They are saying to the world that they are beautiful and confident in themselves. They love the differences in their bodies. To them, beauty is not looking anorexic but being the best human being that they can be.

What good is it to have a beautiful face and an attitude of a rattlesnake? We have all seen and know people with these unattractive qualities. True beauty is when we possess all the qualities and attributes of God and can see the same in others.

Too beautiful for words is what we are. God loved us so much so that He knows every intricate part of our bodies. He knows the number of hairs on our heads. Only someone that loves you would know these intimate things about you. Kimberly Smith waited too late to see that she was naturally beautiful from the start, but you have a chance today to realize that true beauty does not come by the cutting of the knife but comes from within you.

Chapter Twenty-one

Wonderfully Made

I will praise thee; for I am fearfully and wonderfully made: marvellous
are thy works; and that my soul knoweth right well (Psalms 139:14
KJV).

Have you ever considered the genetic makeup of your body? God put
so much thought into creating you. He took so much care into placing
every organ, limb, and strand of hair in its proper place. And when He finished, He thought about what color to make your skin, your eyes, the tex-
ture of your hair, and the details of your facial features. King David thought
about that when he considered how marvelous God had made him. So
much so, that he began to praise his Creator:

You made all the delicate, inner parts of my body, and knit them together
in my mother's womb. Thank you for making me so wonderfully com-
plex! It is amazing to think about. Your workmanship is marvelous—
and how well I know it. You were there while I was being formed in
utter seclusion! You saw me before I was born and scheduled each day of
my life before I began to breathe. Every day was recorded in your book!
(Psalms 139:13-16 TLB).

I'm like King David. When I begin to think about how God formed
and made me, it blows my mind. To think about how He hid me in my
mother's womb until He was finished developing me takes my breath away.
No words can describe His awesomeness. No matter how scientists try to
figure out how to clone humans, God made only one of you. And when He

returns you to the dust that you came from, there will never be another you. You can have children that are the spitting image of you or even a twin, but there's only one you.

Just knowing how God knitted us together should be enough to build up our self-confidence. How He lovingly constructed all the delicate parts of our bodies and fit them perfectly together should be enough for us to see how beautiful we truly are.

Imagine in your mind for a second how God must have felt when He looked and saw the dirt lying on the ground. I believe that He thought it was the most beautiful dirt from which to form His most precious creation.

We seem to look at our birthmarks, scars, and moles on our bodies as flaws and imperfections that need to be removed. But, when God made us, He knew where He wanted those so-called defects to be placed. They may be a nuisance to us, but they are beautiful to God.

When I was young, I thought that people that had beauty moles (moles above the upper lip or on the face) were so beautiful. I would say to myself, *When I grow up, I am going to get me a beauty mole.* But as I got older, I found out that many of the people that had these moles thought that they were the most hideous things on their faces and wanted them removed. It's funny what one person sees as beautiful, another views as unattractive.

I remember when I first met my husband, and I saw this huge birthmark on the side of his neck. Overlooking it was not easy, but as we kept dating, I noticed the birthmark less and less. That goes to show how we judge people by the way they look, instead of what's in their hearts. I could have let a good man slip through my fingers by looking at the outward appearance.

King David was speechless when it came to the human body. From the crown of his head to the bottom of his feet, he was in total awe of how his Creator took special care to knit him together. With all of King David's worldly flaws, he believed that he was perfectly made. When he thought about the way God had made him, he knew that words could not describe the process.

He praised God further by saying, *"You saw me before I was born and scheduled each day of my life before I began to breathe"* (Psalm 139:16 TLB). Only a sovereign God could know the amount of days that we have here on earth. Only the original designer would know what He's going to create before He does it.

King David thanked God for making him so wonderfully complex. In other words, he was saying that the Creator made man in such a way that to think about how He did it boggles the mind. Scientists are amazed each day at how the human body functions and how it is put together. Many of them will never acknowledge God as the original designer but give the credit to evolution for causing man to originate from an explosion.

David said, *"It is amazing to think about"* (Psalm 139:14 TLB). It is amazing because no one has the ability to take dust and form one of the most beautiful creatures that has ever walked this earth. The way the anatomy of the human body is put together is astonishing—how God put so much thought into how each bone would connect and where to place the organs that keep us alive. It's mind-blowing to sit back and think about how God made us wonderfully complex and unique. Although all humans live by the spirit of God, He put something different and unique in each of us.

How precious it is, Lord, to realize that you are thinking about me constantly! I can't even count how many times a day your thoughts turn towards me. And when I wake in the morning, you are still thinking of me! (Psalms 139:17-18 TLB).

There is no greater feeling than knowing that someone loves and cares about us. God did not create us for His amusement but because of love. No matter how our faces become filled with wrinkles and no matter how much our outward beauty fades, we will still be God's most treasured possessions. When our bodies no longer stand erect but bend with age, God still sees the beauty in us, even though man only sees old age and a shell of what once was. Man believes that beauty fades with age, but to God we become more beautiful as time passes.

I cannot begin to put into words how awesome it is that God would put so much thought into little old me. As each second, minute, hour, day, month, and year passes, I am constantly on my heavenly Father's mind. Although time will take away my earthly beauty, He still sees past the outer exterior and sees what matter most—my inner beauty.

For older women that are married, when father time, gravity, and wrinkles come to claim their shapely bodies, some husbands will trade them in for a twenty-something version. This is because they fell in love with the outer appearance and never saw the inner beauty that their wives possess. Can you imagine living and sleeping with someone for years, and waking up one day to find out that they were only there for what you looked like physically? Many can walk away from a marriage of thirty years because it was based on physical attraction and nothing more.

God is with us for the long haul. It does not matter what we look like when we are sixty or seventy years old. We are always on His mind, and He never stops loving us, even when time wears on us. Only humans turn their love on and off because of what they see physically.

God's Validation

Who wants to live their entire lives without anyone ever telling them that they are beautiful or that they are valuable to them? There is no need to wait on the approval of others when God has validated you already. He finalized His love and your beauty when He breathed a part of Himself into you. Although it's nice to hear that you are beautiful from others from time to time, do not get caught into the trap of thinking you have to hear it from someone else to believe it. Waiting to hear those words will cause you to lose yourself.

When you surrender your power over to others, that submission keeps you defeated because you waited for them to tell you what you want to hear. True, you are wonderfully made; God has already validated those claims. Do you know that God delighted Himself in creating you? When looking in the mirror, have you ever thought about what God was thinking when He made you or, why did He shape your eyes, lips, and face the way that He did?

But now, O Lord, thou art our father; we are the clay, and thou our potter; and we all are the work of thy hand (Isaiah 64:8 KJV).

Imagine how God had His hands wrapped around us and sculpted us into something exquisite. Just to know that we are the work of His hands is astonishing. Clay or dirt in its original state is plain and not very beautiful. But when the potter is finished molding and shaping it, the earthy material becomes something beautiful. The clay becomes valuable when it takes on another form. And so are we to God. We started out as dirt, but in our finished form we became living, breathing humans. Just like the potter, God knew what He was going to do with the dirt before He created man.

This should give you goose bumps to know that a potter takes special care when he begins to make his vessels. He starts out slow and ends slow, so that there will be no flaws in his finished product. Not only does he want to sit back and admire it, he wants others to do the same.

God did the same when He worked on us. He took special care as to how He wanted the color of our hair, eyes, and skin. He knows that beauty comes in a variety of shades and colors. God wanted to make sure that we would love and appreciate the uniqueness in each other. But Satan spoke and began showing others how their differences would make them superior to others. Therefore, the harmony that was supposed to exist between all men was broken by inferiority, oppression, injustice, and slavery.

Being confident of this very thing, that he which hath begun a good work in you will perform it until the day of Jesus Christ (Philippians 1:6 KJV).

Paul was letting the Philippians know that God is able to complete what He had started in them. What He started was a good work. God does not waste His time making junk. If you feel worthless or unattractive, maybe you need to realize the great work that God has done on the inside of you.

He said, *"You should be confident that of this very thing, that he which hath begun a good work in you will perform it."* You must know who you are in Christ; and if you know this, then you also know that God has already performed that good work in you. And, you must believe in what He has done in you so that you will not allow others to make you feel incomplete.

For he knoweth our frame; he remembereth that we are dust" (Psalms 103:14 KJV).

God framed man in such a way that there is none other on earth that is constructed like him. We are the only creatures that God touched with His hands; everything else was spoken into existence. Some animals resemble humans, but none that are erected upright. Sooner or later, they will have to return to all fours as they were created to do.

I pray that you remember that God had you on His mind before the earth was formed and that He knew exactly how He wanted you to look.

It's time for you to recognize the beauty that's within you and know that God designed you in such a special way. Words cannot begin to describe how fearfully and wonderfully made you are.

Chapter Twenty-two

Exceeding the Expectations of Others

Jesus saith unto them, Did ye never read in the scriptures, The stone which the builders rejected, the same is become the head of the corner: this is the Lord's doing, and it is marvellous in our eyes? (Matthew 21:42 KJV).

Are you one of the millions of people walking around today feeling worthless? Did you know that no one that God called and used to fulfill a specific task in the Bible met the expectations of others? Jesus, the King of kings, was born and grew up in poverty. King David was a shepherd. Moses, whom God used to lead the children of Israel from bondage out of the land of Egypt, had a speech impediment (he stuttered). Barrack was a coward and God used a woman to help give him courage to fight in battle. There were also prostitutes and adulterous women that became loyal followers of Jesus. And let's not forget the apostle Peter, who was quick-tempered and spoke before he thought.

Exceeding the expectations of others is what all of these men and women did in the Bible, but it does not have to end with them. Some men and women in our generation too have overcome the negative image that others had of them. We grew up with people that we thought would have ended up in jail or on the streets just by how they behaved. We believed that they would never amount to anything because their lives were so corrupt. However, God had other plans for their lives. He made them upstanding citizens and mentors in their communities.

What I love about God is that He has a funny way of turning the negativity of others into something positive. He placed the will to survive in all of us, and many will take that drive and determination and turn their lives into success stories. With God, where you find yourself at one particular moment does not matter. He has the power to turn you into one of the most influential people in the world. Man is the one that says, "Three strikes and you are out," but God says, "Not so, you are just warming up." With God, all you need is faith and determination, and the sky will be the limit for you.

Many people have found themselves in situations where people have thought less of them because of the things they have done. But God never used people who had it all together—He always used the underdog to fulfill His promises. Nobody expects much from the underdog, so you place your money on the sure bet, confident that he or she will win. God loves to use underdogs to accomplish His will. He knows that the sure bet is pumped up in self. The sure bet believes that it's his or her own abilities that are getting that individual ahead. In contrast, underdogs are humble and modest. Therefore, God can use them because they know that it takes faith, drive, and determination from within to help them push forward.

God wants you to succeed in everything that you do. When man says you can't, God says you can. Most people see the potential in you, but due to jealousy and envy, they set their plans in motion to destroy your dreams. They want to keep you frustrated so that the seed that God has placed in you will never grow.

We all have a story to tell about the people that Satan placed in our lives to keeps us from moving forward. But, we must first recognize that it's Satan. Many will never know that it was he that put traps in their paths. He wants our lives to remain at a standstill.

Think about it like this: Satan will never tell you anything good about yourself. So, when you hear that you are a failure or question the wisdom of going back to school to further your education when pessimistic thoughts tell you that you will never find a job in that field, know that Satan is trying to distract you. He does not want you to better your life. His job is to keep you stagnant.

Jesus, our Lord and Savior, exceeded others' expectations of Him. People looked down on Him because of where He was born and who His parents were. But Jesus knew one thing: He must be about His Father's business. He did not let what others thought about Him delay what He was called to do. We must not allow family and friends to stop us from fulfilling our destinies. They can make us feel foolish, dumb, and incapable of greatness.

Sadly, it's the people that we are closest to that most often try to sabotage our dreams. A stranger will encourage you to keep pressing forward before most family members or friends will. A stranger has nothing to gain or lose by telling you that you can do whatever you attempt. The people that are closest to you are the ones holding your head under water. They know that if you ever reach the surface, you will see the plans that God has for your life. Many are drowning and want to take you under with them. Why would a loved one or a trusted friend conceal the truth from you? It always goes back to two little words that have so much power and influence over people—envy and jealousy. They are usually the top motives. No one is exempt. If it has not happened to you yet, keep living!

The people in Jesus' day suffered from the same problems. Jesus knew who He was, and He was not going to let the devil tell Him otherwise. We must take the same stand when trying to exceed others' expectations of us. God sees nothing but success and great potential when He looks at us. However, we must believe the same about ourselves in order to become that success. The fact that God sees our potential is not enough because He saw it in the murderers, drug addicts, and thieves. They did not see the vision for themselves and took the easy way out, succumbing to what the devil said that they were—failures.

If Jesus had let those negative influences stop Him from fulfilling His destiny, where would we be today? We certainly would not be enjoying the freedom that we have today if all the great people that fought for human rights had said, "Let someone else lose his or her life. I'm not standing up for that cause. It's not my business."

Exceeding the expectations of others means never giving up, no matter how people speak against you or try holding you back. I was always told, "Anything worth having is worth fighting for." Many individuals are satisfied with sitting on the sidelines watching someone else win the race. Don't allow their laziness to cause you to become a spectator too. Get in the race; be all that God has called you to be.

Jesus is the ultimate example. He set the standard to exceed. He was born in a feeding trough, worked as a carpenter, and was laughed at and scorned. However, He fulfilled what He was called to do, no matter what was required or how badly it hurt. He persevered through it all to be the

Savior that God anointed Him to be. He suffered through it all because He knew that you and I would be coming generations later and would need an example to follow.

Who would have thought that God would use a shepherd (King David), one of the lowest positions, to rise up to be a king and generations later send the Savior of the world as one of his descendants? God is so awesome that He used the least expected to save the world from sin. That alone should tell you that God can do marvelous things through you as well. Do not count yourself as useless.

King David was a young boy when God anointed him to be king. Jesse, David's father, thought for sure that Samuel, a prophet of the Lord, would anoint one of his older boys. God chose David, not for the boy he was at that moment, but for the man he would become in the future. God saw David's courage, knowing that he would need it in the future to defeat Goliath. He knew that King David would continually praise Him, even when faced with tragedy and running for his life from King Saul.

Your age or who you are at any given moment does not keep you from exceeding the expectations of others. God uses those with willing hearts. If your family told you that you will never amount to anything, prove them wrong! Does it make you a failure that you had a child out of wedlock and people said that you will always be dependent on government assistance? Prove them wrong and go back to school to improve your life. No one can keep you from going forward but you.

Becoming Role Models

I was impressed years ago when I was watching television and saw three young black men that had been friends since childhood (Sampson Davis, George Jenkins, and Rameck Hunt). They made a pact with each other that they would become doctors when they graduated from high school. They kept their promise to one another and did just that. These friends did not let their environments suck them into becoming statistics of failure.

According to the *Seattle Times*, the three doctors said that they were accustomed to seeing drug dealings, muggings, and car thefts. I'm sure that they had to encourage one another to keep pressing forward when things looked bleak. Although they practiced as physicians in different fields, they became what they said they would. They exceeded others' expectations of them. If you were to ask them how friends and family reacted when they heard of their pact, I bet most of them thought that they would never make it because of where they grew up and who they were.

Other friends thought they were crazy. The only black doctor any of them knew of was the fictional character Bill Cosby played on TV. Some teachers even told them they wouldn't succeed. However, they encouraged each other that they would succeed.

Who would have thought that their dreams would become a reality? One day, Davis and Hunt were trying to cut class to avoid a substitute teacher. Even then, God was putting them on the path to fulfilling their destinies. While cutting class, they slipped into the library where a health and science seminar was being conducted. It was Jenkins who persuaded the other two that they were destined to become doctors. All it took was for one to see the vision and to get the others to believe that it was possible. Now these three young men are living the American dream, all because they did not allow the negative forces around them to pollute what God had put into them—a dream.

These three young men give back, by encouraging others that they can do the same. The *Seattle Times* says, "Jenkins and Davis still live in Newark's inner city, not because they have to, but so other troubled youngsters can find role models just down the street."

God is so awesome, and I am thankful each day to know that I have a part of Him living inside of me. He inspires us to become all that we can be; just knowing that He's always there to catch us when we fall is amazing.

Yes, these young men were laughed at for making good grades and because they were the product of single-parent homes, but they defied the odds. They saw themselves bigger than their environments and became what God saw them as—doctors, roles models, and leaders in their communities.

When we do not achieve our dreams the first time we try, often others want to say, "I told you so." Do not listen to those discouraging words. We may not succeed the first time, but we must keep trying until something happens. The people that have excelled at what they do will tell us that it took more than one try to get where they wanted to be. Some dreams don't come true overnight; it takes hard work and determination to see them manifested in our lives. When we reach our goals, no one can take them away. As the saying goes, "Nothing in life is free." If you want it badly enough, then you have to earn it.

Using Our Weaknesses for His Glory

Moses raised another objection to God: "Master, please, I don't talk well. I've never been good with words, neither before nor after you spoke to me. I stutter and stammer." God said, "And who do you think made the human mouth? And who makes some mute, some, deaf, some sighted, some blind? Isn't it I, God? So, get going. I'll be right there with you— with your mouth! I'll be right there to teach you what to say" (Exodus 4:10-12 MSG).

It's amazing how God will take the things that we think are handicaps and use them for His glory. When we are weak, He is strong. God does not use perfect people to do His will. We see Him every day using those who have flaws or imperfections to excel.

Moses was not eloquent in speech, but that did not stop God from using him to set His people free from slavery under the Egyptians government. When we allow others to point out our so-called handicaps, we begin to look at ourselves in a negative way. God wanted to show Moses that He could use whomever He chose to deliver His people, and that he was the right man for the job.

God told Moses that He would be with him. He used Moses' brother Aaron to speak for him, but that does not mean that God could not have taken the stutter from his mouth. When Moses came face to face with Pharaoh, God blessed him to speak and stand with authority.

Many times we miss our calling because we are afraid of what people might think of us. What if our forefathers would have allowed their physical appearances to stop them from fulfilling their destinies? "I'm a paraplegic; I cannot run for president" or "I am a black man; I will be killed if I stand up for civil rights." God has so much greatness deep down inside of us all, but we have allowed what others see as handicaps to stop us.

We allow poverty, skin color, weight, and other areas to keep us from being all that we can be. What if James Earl Jones would have allowed his stuttering to stop him from acting? The world would have never been blessed by his prolific acting skills. He pushed forward and went against the norm; he went on to become one of the greatest actors of our times.

That is what happens when people see themselves as God does. Their dreams are right at the tip of their tongues; all they have to do is speak them into existence.

Faith was required of Moses to believe that he could be the one to get Pharaoh to set God's people free. After having many excuses, he finally believed what God told him about himself. Once you believe what God has told you, the devil in hell cannot stop you. Yes, the naysayers will still be there, but so will God. That is why Moses had so much conviction each time he stood before Pharaoh. In my mind, I can see Pharaoh saying, "Moses has some nerve coming before me when he cannot speak fluently." Your mockers may say the same about you. They believe because of their position and your handicap that you have no right to speak to them with such conviction and authority. Moses asked God a very important question.

And Moses said unto God, Who am I, that I should go unto Pharaoh, and that I should bring forth the children of Israel out of Egypt? And God said unto Moses, "I AM THAT I AM:" and he said, "Thus shalt thou say unto the children of Israel, I AM hath sent me unto you" (Exodus 3:11, 14).

Just know that if you stand firm, God will be there to see you through to the other side. He promised to never leave you nor forsake you. God will keep His Word because He knows the potential that lies within you. He knew you before you were born. Before your parents ever thought about having a child, God knew the qualities and capabilities that He would put inside of you.

Moses may have been born with a speech impediment, but that did not limit who he was in God. Amazingly, God can take what man has tossed aside and use it for His glory. If He could make a jackass talk, surely He can make a man with impaired speech do the same. *"And the Lord opened the mouth of the ass, and she said unto Balaam, What have I done unto thee, that thou hast smitten me these three times?"* (Numbers 22:28 KJV). Only God can take a man with a disability and turn Him into one of the most memorable and influential men in Bible history.

My question to you is, what handicaps are you allowing to keep you from exceeding the expectations of others? If you look at all the people that God used in the Bible, whether good or bad, you will find that He never used perfect people, only those that made themselves available. Prove others wrong and allow God to put you in places that others thought were impossible.

Chapter Twenty-three

Finding the Courage To Stand

One day she summoned Barak (son of Abinoam), who lived in Kedesh, in the land of Naphtali, and said to him, "The Lord God of Israel has commanded you to mobilize ten thousand men from the tribes of Naphtali and Zebulun. Lead them to Mount Tabor to fight King Jabin's mighty army with all his chariots, under General Sisera's command. The Lord says, 'I will draw them to the Kishon River, and you will defeat them there.'" "I'll go, but only if you go with me!" Barak told her (Judges 4:6-8).

God is no respecter of persons. He used a coward to fulfill His plans to defeat Jabin and his army. Barak was a man of war, but during one battle, he lost his courage to fight. God had to prove to him through a woman, Deborah, that He would be victorious.

Many of us have this coward syndrome as well. When people know that someone is weak, it makes it that much easier for them to control that individual. They will tell that person negative things about him or her to keep that individual under their control. They will always dominate situations in the relationship because they know the subdued person will not protest.

Having someone in your life that you have confidence in gives you a sense of security. Barak had that in Deborah. Although he would go into battle with ten thousand men, he still needed the encouragement of Deborah. He knew that she was a prophetess of the Lord. He believed in the words that she spoke to him because they came straight from the mouth of God.

Many of us are encouraged by what others speak into our lives. We excel in life and want more for ourselves because of their encouragement. It's a good feeling to know that we can conquer anything just by hearing positive words that are being spoken into our lives.

Positive encouragement works just the same as negative encouragement. When others believe in you, you feel that you can achieve anything. On the other hand, when people doubt your abilities, sometimes it makes you second-guess yourself. Words influence and shape our everyday lives.

I pray that you go out and conquer your fears and find the courage to stand. Trust what God has put in you. *"For God hath not given us the spirit of fear; but of power, and of love, and of a sound mind"* (2 Timothy 1:7 KJV). Do not wimp out like Barak so that you feel you need someone else's faith and courage before you believe. God has already given you the victory; all you have to do now is go, seek, and conquer. He's all that you need. It's time for you to cross over into the enemies' territory, knowing that God will give you the strength to stand.

What others think about you is not important, but what you believe or think about yourself is vital. Stop moping around and see yourself through the eyes of God—standing strong. Become victorious in whatever you want to do. If you never try, then you will never know what the outcome will be. God knows your limitations, but it is up to you to expect and want more for yourself.

People that are defeated want you to stay the same. Look at the people that keep putting stumbling blocks in your way. Are they where they want to be in life? Have they fulfilled any of their dreams? Are they successful? Are they constantly speaking insults and negativity against your plans in life? Do you know why? Failure begets failure. Probably nothing has worked out in their lives, and they do not want to see your plans come to fruition either so they set traps to ruin your chances of succeeding.

Look at the lives of people that speak positive words into your life. Are they confident, although they have flaws? Are they encouraging you not to give up on your dreams? Do you know why? They know that what God has for them no man can hinder or remove. They have no problem helping you succeed because they know that God will make room for their gifts and talents. A person that knows who they are in Christ has no problem in building up someone else.

People that try to keep you down are always worried that someone is going to steal their position. This shows that they really do not know who they are in Christ. If they knew who they were in Him, they would understand that God has many gifts, talents, and blessings for us all. They would also know that you do not have to shatter another person's dreams to fulfill or succeed at theirs. Only people that are unsure of themselves attempt to destroy others. Knowing who you are is so important. If you do, then no amount of trash talk will stop you from becoming what you were destined to be. Often people allow the devil to come and destroy their good work because they were not able to see past his tricks and manipulation.

Speak Positive Words

Jesus had the opportunity to witness and show mercy to one woman that was believed to be a prostitute and two others that were called adulterous women. Although Jesus knew what kinds of women they were, He did not criticize them as others did. The men that were benefiting from one of these women's services were the same men pointing their fingers at her and wanting her to be stoned to death.

Jesus sought opportunities such as these to show mercy and to offer a better way of living for these three women. What if He would have been like many of us? We turn up our noses and look down on people, instead of showing compassion and seeing what they will eventually become. Rather, we often focus on who they are at that present moment.

When we see people that we think do not measure up to our expectations, do we look at them with contempt and disgust? Do we witness and talk to the person that looks successful but turn our backs to the ones that look down and out? We often make excuses for why we treat them differently, saying, "They do not want any better for themselves, so why bother." Did you take the time to ask? Do you know the reason why they are in that predicament? We assume things about people before we get to know them.

At times, life serves us heavy blows or setbacks that knock us off our feet, but we should not give up on each other. Find out a person's story before we make up our minds about them. Poverty, prostitution, and adultery never stopped anyone from succeeding in life. These are minor setbacks that can be fixed, but a judgmental heart needs much more work because it keeps us from seeing the possibilities in others.

Jesus saw faithfulness and thankfulness in these women. Yes, they were walking in sin when they met Jesus. However, He did not judge or ridicule them for the way they were living. Only a compassionate heart can look past a person's present state and say, "I'll show you a better way to live." Jesus did just that. When men wanted to stone one of these women for being caught in the act of adultery, Jesus said, "*He that is without sin among you, let him first cast a stone at her*" (John 8:7 KJV).

We often cannot see sin in ourselves, but invariably we can notice it in others. Jesus knew that the men that wanted her to be stoned to death were many of her clients. They wanted her to pay with her life while they went unpunished for their sins.

Jesus delivered this woman from the cynical men and from the life that she was living. Jesus saw the potential in her and realized that all she needed was encouragement to turn her life around for the better.

Now is the time to stop being judgmental towards others and start speaking uplifting words into their lives. People can go further in life if we stop paralyzing them with our critical spirits. God blessed us and helped us to become successful so that we can show others that they can do likewise.

Many theologians believed that the woman with the alabaster box was a prostitute. Whatever her occupation was, she was more courteous towards Jesus than the Pharisees that had invited Him into their home for a dinner party. In the Bible days, a woman in her field would not dare come to a public party where so-called dignitaries were present. But, she had a need and she knew that there was a man there that could cleanse her of her sins. She did what the Pharisees did not do when inviting Jesus into their homes—she washed His feet (see Matthew 26:1-13).

In those days, it was the custom that when you were invited to someone's home that the host would wash your feet. They knew that you had traveled through the sandy dessert and mud. The Pharisees did neither because they had another agenda for inviting Jesus into their home.

As this woman's tears fell upon Jesus' feet, she began to take her hair and wipe them. She also broke her expensive perfume to anoint Jesus. We seem to think that it would be the person that had the most that would have honored or showed respect towards Him. But it was the least of them that reverenced Jesus. This woman took what was valuable to her and used it on Jesus. In return, He told her of all her sins—whatever they were— were forgiven by Him.

We too can learn from this story because it's often the people that have the least that will share all that they have with you. Those that have are sometimes only concerned with holding on to their possessions because they have other devious plans in mind. They only want to hang out with you to get information. The Pharisees had their own little plans for Jesus, but this woman with the alabaster box foiled their plans. Jesus used her situation to teach them a lesson.

They had the opportunity to show hospitality but refused to do so. Jesus used a woman with a scandalous occupation to teach them the value of serving others. What good is it to possess great things but snub your nose at those that can benefit from your help the most?

Mary Magdalene was a woman possessed with several demons. People looked at her as an outcast. She also found the courage to stand. Mary became one of Jesus' most loyal followers. She was so faithful towards Jesus that she followed Him when the Roman soldier was taking Him to the cross. Along with others, she went to Jesus' grave to embalm His body, when the men were to scared to do so.

No matter what may have had you bound in the past, the possibilities for your success are endless. If God can take a prostitute and turn her into one of His most trusted followers, just think what He can do in you. The ball is in your court; find the courage to stand when others have dismissed you.

Peter was an impetuous person. He popped off at the mouth quite often, speaking before thinking. He was certainly not the obvious choice of person for God to use as His mouthpiece for something great. The apostle Peter went on to be one of the greatest apostles, taking God's Word to all men. Jesus told Peter, *"And I say also unto thee, That thou art Peter, and upon this rock I will build my church; and the gates of hell shall not prevail against it"* (Matthew 16:18 KJV). This was before Peter's spiritual transformation.

Peter's problem still existed after becoming one of Jesus' most trusted disciples. He still struggled with accepting people that were different from him. But God used him to teach the very people whom he considered to be inferior. With God, the things that we have problems with are the very things that He will use to bring us into submission to Him.

God has a sense of humor. I remember watching a talk show years ago. They had a gentleman that was an ex-member of the Ku Klux Klan that had turned his life over to Christ. He said that the same people that he had so much hate for were the same people that God had sent him to preach of His saving grace. Can you imagine what those people thought? This was a person that was often seen on television spreading his message of hate and genocide of another race.

Although Peter was not preaching hate, he still had his hang-ups towards people that were different from him. This was reinforced in him since childhood and took a loving God to remove it.

It pays to be careful when God has set you apart to be an encourager and motivator to others. It can be like a double-edged sword. It will cut you if you do not handle it properly. Practice what you teach because people are watching and waiting for you to slip. God has placed you here on earth to be the light that shines brightly into someone's life.

Finding the courage to stand should be our motivation when conquering the naysayers in our lives. Many people are betting against us. They are praying that we fall by the wayside. We must find the courage within to keep pressing forward because the race is not given to the swift or the strong but to the ones that endure to the end.

The time is now to break free from Satan's stronghold. Believe in yourself and the gifts and talents that God has placed in you. Be all that you can be because you have only one life to live. Once you have come to the end of it, you can truly say that you found the courage to stand against every obstacle placed in your life.

Chapter Twenty-four

Words Can't Bring Me Down

When you know who you are in Christ, no matter how someone tries to bring you down with hurtful or insulting words, it won't work. No weapon that is formed against you—even the weapon of the tongue—will not prosper. Prayer will give you the stability to stand against any verbal attacks from the devil.

I thank God for inspiring this chapter because we all know that words can cut like a knife, especially when the one that is doing the insulting does it with the intent to harm. Words are like weights; if we listen to them long enough, they will cause us to lose our balance.

The injured person brings life to those words when they are rehearsed over and over in his or her mind. Once those words take root, that person, in turn, speaks mean and hurtful words towards someone else. Yes, you can say that words are like a boomerang. They have a way of coming back around; either those words will lift you up or they will tear you down.

I was always told, "Never let a person know what your weaknesses are." If you reveal them, others may take advantage of you. Just watch how a conversation turns when you are talking to someone that you think is close to you but they really aren't. They will find the thing that you hate about yourself the most and attack you with it. Whether it's your lack of confidence or your looks, they will use it as a weapon.

You may want to believe that everyone that is close to you wants what is best for you, but that's not true in many cases. Watch a person's reaction and listen to their conversation. They are the first two giveaways in knowing who is for you and who is against you. Their words will become cold and bitter, sometimes downright mean and hurtful. Why? Jealousy causes their words to become nasty and vindictive. They never have an encouraging word to say.

Christina Aguilera sang a song called "Beautiful" about this. The song says you were doing just fine until you allowed someone's words to discourage you. You were confident and self-assured until that one person's demeaning words made you feel differently. As a result, you now question everything about yourself.

My heart goes out to our young children that are growing up in this superficial world described in the song above. They are fragile and insecure. The smallest negative words will cause them to have low self-esteem. They worry about things that I never had to concern myself with as a child. Social pressures are a concern. The need to belong is causing them to do things that they do not want to do.

For most young adults, words are like sticks of dynamite that are ready to go off at any second. They need encouragement because they are one another's worst enemies. The painful words that they say to each other are like writing that is etched in stone—sometimes the pain is permanent. They believe what someone their own age tells them rather than their parents. Many young adults feel a parent only tells them what they want to hear, but their peers are telling them the truth, whether it's positive or negative.

Our kids are suffering from the words of others. To make matters worse, they now have to deal with cyber-bullying. These malicious and vindictive words coming across the Internet are holding our children hostage within their own homes with no one there to rescue them. No one is there because the children are afraid to let their parents know what is happening. A young child committed suicide because of taunting words from an adult disguising herself as a teenager on the MySpace website. The adult told this young child that the world would be better off without her. Words are powerful, especially in a young child's life.

One word can make people believe that they can conquer the world. One word spoken in love can get a child off the streets. One kind word can make a difference in someone's life. Will you be that one person to speak words of encouragement into a hurting heart? Will you be the father to say, "You are not stupid, and you can do anything you set out to do." Will you be the father to wrap his arms around his son and say, "Real men do cry and show their emotions"? You are not a wimp when you possess these qualities, for these are the qualities of God.

A Destiny To Fulfill

King David danced before the Lord when the Ark of the Covenant was found (see 2 Samuel 6:14). His wife was disgusted when she saw this act and began to say, "Look how he embarrasses himself before the people." David could have let this ruin his day, but he did not allow words to discourage him. He kept right on dancing. Never let anyone ruin your day. If that person wants to be miserable, let him or her do that without you, and don't let critical words hinder you.

We should do as David did when others ridicule us about why we act the way we do. Their ignorance should not stop us from being happy. The devil does not want us to be excited about anything. He will put someone in our way to steal our joy. That is his job—to keep us depressed, second-guessing, and unsure of ourselves.

Words could have stopped Jesus from going to Calvary, but they did not. Words could have stopped Saul (now the apostle Paul) on the Damascus road, but they did not. Words could have stopped blind Bartimaeus from crying out to Jesus and the harlot, Rahab, from helping the twelve spies or the disciples because of their educational background, but they did not. All these people had the same things in common with us—they had a destiny to fulfill.

Satan's job is to stop that destiny, that dream, and your ambitions. And words are the weapons that he will use to accomplish this. Wise up and recognize who is sending those attacks. People aren't just saying those hurtful words because that is their desire; the enemy is speaking through them to stop you. It's very important that you learn this before you allow those words to control your thinking. If they can manipulate your thought process, they will dominate your entire being—mind, body, and soul.

We all are tempted to give up during trying times, but God has given us the ability to encourage ourselves. When those moments come, call upon that one Word that He has placed inside us all—Jesus. Speak His name out loud, so that the enemy will know that he has no control over us and that Jesus has made us victorious over any crippling words that Satan tried to speak into our minds.

Pick up the Word of God and read what it says you are in Him. Do not believe the words of the enemy. His words were meant to bring you down and keep you there. Any negative words that are spoken in your life are from the devil himself. God's Word will always motivate and rejuvenate you. God's Word will cause you to believe that you can do the impossible. His Word will cause you to soar like an eagle. God's anointed Word will build you up, not destroy you.

Yes, words do have power and we give them control over our lives when we accept their crushing impact. As I write this chapter, lives are being shaped and formed by the words that are spoken from someone today, whether for good or bad. People are being controlled mentally by words that they have allowed to enter into their lives.

What are some of the repercussions of allowing negative words to shape and form your life?

- Believing and conforming to what's said about you.
- Believing that something is wrong with you.
- Living life below your potential.
- Always second-guessing yourself.
- Never fulfilling your destiny.

God wants so much more for us. We must stop allowing others to steal what God has put inside of us. He has put creativity and uniqueness inside of us all. He did not place it inside of us just to allow the devil and his cohorts to steal it. God wants us to live above our potential. The word *potential* is one that says I have the possibilities of making it, but God's Word says that I am more than a conqueror. I'm not just going to make it; I will take my life, my happiness, and joy back by force. I will become victorious over whatever I aspire to be.

We have allowed hurtful words from others to cause us to bury our dreams. Our dreams lie desolate in the spirit realm, waiting on us to retrieve them. Dreams die within us because someone's deadly words have killed them. The tragedy is that we never tried to revive those dreams. They could have been resuscitated if we had fought to keep them alive. My pastor uses a term called, "Dream Busters." These are people that are placed in our lives by Satan to punch holes in our dreams.

Can you imagine all the people that have lived and died, never seeing their dreams come to fruition? Just think of all the inventions, songs, books, and businesses that will never be known because someone told them that their dreams were a waste of time. They listened to the wrong people—the Dream Busters. Satan often attaches them to you so that you will give up on fulfilling your dreams.

In Pastor Joel Osteen's book, *Become a Better You,* he says, "The grave-yard is one of the riches places on earth." Do you know why? Because of all the dreams that never had the chance to be born. Someone in those graves allowed the Dream Busters to kill them. These people lived their entire lives never fulfilling their destinies. It is possible to live and never do what God has placed you on this earth to do. Words have been the stumbling block that have caused many not to live above their potential. Do not become that person that lay on his or her deathbed wondering how life would have been if he or she had followed the path that Christ had ordained. Life is full of could've, should've, and would've. Do not let one of these regrets be yours.

Being All We Can Be

Our own words will keep us defeated as well. We need to be careful of what we say and think about ourselves because we give our words life when we speak them.

Words will not defeat me. I will not allow negative conversation to come from my mouth. I will become the person that God has created me to be. I will not let my gifts go to the grave unfulfilled and unknown to the world. I will not allow others to influence me with their opinions. I am going places in this life, even if I have to go alone. I want more than just to exist. I want to fulfill my destiny.

If you read these words out loud, they sound good; but do you believe them? Or are they just words on a page to you? As soon as you close this book, don't close your mind to all that God has to offer.

Whether you are young or old, today is the day to start being who God has created you to be. It is never too late to follow your dreams. Stop allowing others to put an age or time limit on when you should have your dreams accomplished. Jesus told us, *"Occupy till I come"* (Luke 19:13 KJV). That means that each of us should be doing something until He returns or when He calls us home to be with Him. He did not leave us here to do nothing.

Be the person that you know that you can be. Do not allow the environment you come from hinder you. Do not allow your neighborhood friends that are on the street corner prevent you from going forth. They may laugh at you when you share your dreams and goals with them, but be the one to break the cycle and give those that are watching an example to follow. Their words may hurt, but use them as a motivational tool to get you where you need to be.

For those that are mentally strong, negative words are not obstacles in your life. These people use those words as a driving force to help push them to become the best that they can be. They allow their enemies' sarcastic remarks to be the driving force to their success. People like this are confidant in who they are. They have learned that mean and hateful words are spoken through envy and jealousy. They can distinguish who their real friends are from those who are just hanging around to see them fall.

Breaking Free

Many of us are allowing words to ruin our days before they get started because we meditate and rehearse what has been said about us. We become unable to break free of their stronghold over our thoughts. It's time to rise above the influence of the haters in our lives and tell the devil that he is a liar and his words have no power—not now, not ever—over us.

John 1:1 (KJV) says, *"In the beginning was the Word, and the Word was with God, and the Word was God."* It did not say that in the beginning that your haters have the last say over your life. So, since the Word—Jesus—was there in the beginning, why is it hard for you to believe that He has everything worked out for you since the beginning of time? He saw this present day before you were an embryo in your mother's womb. He knew what He wanted you to become before you knew. Stop allowing others to govern your life. God knows what is best for you.

If depression or a lack of confidence comes over you, look to the hill from which comes your help—Jesus. Call upon Him; I promise that He will answer. When demeaning words from others are clouding your mind, seek refuge in Jesus. He is always right on time. Just when you feel that you cannot go any further, He will be there to pull you through before the attack from the enemy comes.

Many of us were doing just fine until we allowed others into our lives with their poisonous words. Every day was great until we opened up and let the wrong person into our lives to invade our personal space. Now that person has us second-guessing everything that we do.

We all have been there, confident and self-assured, until one little snake slithers into our lives. It comes and turns everything upside down, causing us to lose focus on all the areas in which we once were confident. We have allowed it to bring us down to its level and to keep us from flourishing.

Some examples of this include the woman that was confident in herself before she allowed an abuser into her life, the child that was happy just being a child and now someone has stolen his or her innocence, and the would-be college student that wanted to break the cycle of illiteracy in his family, only to be told that he would not amount to anything since everyone in the family was a high school dropout. Or it could be the preacher that God put a Word in his or her belly, only to be told, "I know what you used to be." All of these people had dreams, but the power of the words of others was spoken into their lives and kept those dreams from becoming a reality. All this goes to show that words can bring us down if we let them.

We need to speak to the situations in our lives. Let them know that words will not bring us down, not today or any other day. We are pressing forth in the things of God, and we refuse to let the devil tell us what we can and cannot be. We must safeguard our hearts and minds so that people will not cause us to carry our dreams to the grave. Stop and listen carefully to the people that we have allowed into our lives. If they begin to speak words of lies and deceit, we will recognize that those are attacks from the devil. Once we realize their motives, then negative, malicious, hateful, and degrading words will not undermine us, and his words won't bring us down today!

Chapter Twenty-five

Free To Be Me

Then shall the dust return to the earth as it was: and the spirit shall re-
turn unto God who gave it. Vanity of vanities, saith the preacher; all is
vanity (Ecclesiastes 12:7-8 KJV).

When this life is over and we have to give an account to our Maker, what will our beauty have profited us? Soon our bodies will return to dust, and what will we have to show for our existence other than that we were once beautiful? What legacy will we leave behind for the next generation? We will have taught them how to make others feel worthless and ashamed of who God created them to be? What lessons will they learn from us?

God made you just the way He wanted you to be. Stop trying to be someone you're not. You should be content with just being yourself. Why should it bother you that others think that you are too big or small or that your nose is too wide or narrow? All that matters is that you love the image that is staring back at you in the mirror.

Happiness is a state of mind and should not come from the approval of others. Instead, happiness should stem from how you feel about yourself. The freedom to be who you are is liberating. Love the skin you are in. Love just being plain old you, not a celebrity that tries to categorize you into their definition of beauty. Yes, they may be attractive, but at what cost—rehab or to live secretly in a mental institution because they cannot cope with the pressures that the entertainment industry has placed on them?

Being free consists of having no restrictions due to race, weight, or physical features. We should care more about people seeing the inward person, rather than what is on the outside. What is on the outside can be deceptive because in many cases it is shallow and fake. Our true beauty shows up when we are not afraid to expose our flaws for all to see.

Who wants to be dressed from head to toe just to live up to some type of image? When all is said and done, no one will remember or care anyway. No one wants to walk around feeling self-conscious about their every move, wondering constantly what others are thinking about them.

When you are free to be yourself, those that are closest to you will not be able to get you off course. Once you have heard what they had to say, let it go into one ear and out the other one. Because of the freedom that you have, you are not willing to be conformed to anyone's image of you.

There will be times in your life when you will have to fight—mentally, not physically—to escape the labels that others will try to place on you. Just know that it will be worth it. When you come from an impoverished neighborhood, that is all many will ever think about you; and they will try to keep you in that particular place. Unlike their vision of you, you see yourself as God sees you. You know and believe that you are entitled to having more than just merely surviving. The three friends that made the pact to become doctors knew and believed that they could have more. They put their plans into action as youth and fulfilled their destinies. They refused to be held captive by anyone's critical thinking or views of them. Yes, you may be criticized for wanting better, but it will be worth the fight. God is your source and strength. With Him on your side, who can stop you from breaking the chains of bondage and walking in your new freedom?

It takes only one person in your family to break the cycle of inferiority and complacency. That one person could be you. Your family history does not stop you from going forward. You stop yourself when you start focusing on all those that have failed. Success stories only happen through determination and hard work. Listening to critical people will keep your story unheard, untold, and unwritten.

We have jailed ourselves with the negative reports from our enemies. We are incarcerated and bound, whipped and defeated by the power that we have given others when we allow them to control how we should think and feel about ourselves.

What if Jesus allowed words to imprison Him? What if He had listened to the lies of the enemy? What if they would have influenced Him to stick with what He knew? The freedom that He gave us came with a price. We should stop selling out to people that could care less about us and enjoy the freedom that Christ bought for us with His life.

There are millions of people that lie awake at night worrying about what others think of them. The "people factor" will be there until the day you die to cause havoc in your life. Their purpose is to stop you from fulfilling and exceeding your potential. If you do not recognize this before it is too late, you will wake up one day and find yourself aged and still trying to please people. Jesus never wasted a moment worrying about people. He knew they were going to do and say mean and malicious things to get Him off track from God's plans. Jesus kept doing those things that were not popular in the people's eyes but were pleasing in God's eyes.

Being free is all about breaking from the standards of others and loving who you are. It is for all those that have tried to associate you with things that were negative. Being yourself is taking a stand against people that have tried to stomp on your dreams and letting them know that they cannot stop what God has ordained. You have finally realized that no matter what group they try to place you in, it will not determine the person that you will eventually become.

God has ordained you for greatness. His words have given you power and the ability to see any hindering spirits that are in your path. The only thing that can get in your way is doubt and unbelief. People at this point in your life should longer be a problem for you. In the preceding chapters you have seen that through the eyes of God, you have been set free from the "people factor." Through God, there is serenity when you need peace from your enemies.

We are living, breathing miracles in the flesh. Jesus knew us by name over two thousand years ago when He gave His life on Calvary. He knew what we were going to become before our feet ever touched earth. Satan also knew it too, and his job was to kill that miracle before it was born. He has planned to kill those miracles in us by using people to poison them with their words of condemnation. If he can get us to destroy each other's self-esteem, then the battle will be won.

Satan will kill you and your dreams by any means necessary. He knew that once you believed that you could rise above your circumstances, he would have trouble on his hands. Satan is placing people at this very moment in your life to destroy your credibility, your peace, and your self-esteem. Do not be caught off guard when people set traps and speak evil against you. Many of them do not want you to rise above the influence of depression and a low self-image. These spirits will take you to a place of no return if you are not spiritually strong. Be smart and get the help that you need through the Word of God. Once these spirits attach themselves to you, it will take the army of the Lord to remove them. Know the people that come into your life, because it could mean the difference between life and death spiritually. Not everyone that calls you friend is what he or she professes to be. Satan has assigned some of them to you to stop you from moving forward so that your dreams can go unfulfilled.

Satan is the mastermind behind low self-esteem, depression, unworthiness, comparing ourselves to others, negativity, and self-hatred. Once we have read what the Word of God says about the people we truly are, we will learn that we are beautiful, uniquely made, and victorious. We are the only living creatures that God made with His hands. That alone should let us know how special we are to Him. Just to know that He shaped our bodies and molded us into something desirable should motivate us to love who God created us to be.

Epilogue

Through the Eyes of God is written to encourage, to motivate, and to inspire everyone. We may not like many of our body parts and see them as flaws, but God loves them. We are the only creatures that He touched with His hands; everything else was spoken into existence.

Yes, there is always room for improvement, but just know that God has made you a unique, one-of-a-kind diamond in the rough. Hold your head up high because God loves you just the way you are. See yourself through His eyes and live the victorious life that was planned for you before the existence of time.

I praise you because I am fearfully and wonderfully made; your works are wonderful, I know that full well (Psalms 139:14 KJV).

About the Author

Sheila L. Jackson is the author of *The Enemy Within* and has penned many articles, such as: "Only the Strong Survive," "Count It All Joy," and "Suffering in Silence." She lives in Shreveport, Louisiana, with her husband, Timothy, and two daughters, Brittany and Amber.

Mrs. Jackson is an anointed speaker, teacher, and writer who utilizes her gifts to meet the need of others. She serves as a missionary in her church and community, carrying the Word of God to those in need of spiritual soul food.

If you enjoyed reading *Through The Eyes of God*, then you will also want to add to your collection, *The Enemy Within*, by Sheila L Jackson. You can purchase your copy at www.sheilaljackson2.com and learn more about the enemy lurking within us all.

Contact Information

To contact Sheila Jackson for book signings
or speaking engagements, you can e-mail her at:
SJ@comcast.net
or visit her website,
www.sheilaljackson2.com.

LaVergne, TN USA
05 December 2009
166081LV00004B/2/P